Marco Island Writers
Stories and Poems
Volume IV

Marco Island Writers Inc.

Contributors:

Marlene Chabot
Dennis Charles
Sara Clay
Vince D'Angelo
Pauline Hayton
Nick Kalvin
Nancy Reges Murvine
Elisabeth Noyes
Virginia Colwell Read
Ellen Redd
Ellen and Fleur-de-Lys Redd
Joanne Ivy Stankievich
Joanne Simon Tailele
Kristine Taylor
Linda Walker
James J. Waltz
Shirley Woolaway

Published by Marco Island Writers Inc
www.marcoislandwritersinc.com

Copyright © 2017 by Marco Island Writers Inc.

ISBN-13: 978-1547249060

Marco Island Writers Inc. dedicates this book to encouraging the joy of reading and writing to all, especially children.

Front Cover Illustration:

The 6-inch tall wood carving known as the Key Marco Cat was discovered in 1896, preserved in a bog, at the north end of Marco Island, then known as Key Marco. The artifact, dating from ca. 800 AD, is attributed to the Calusa Indians, an advanced and powerful tribe living along the southwest coast of Florida.

Visitors to Marco Island museum encounter a human-size bronze sculpture of the Key Marco Cat and inside the museum is a replica of original six-inch wooden figure. The original is at the Smithsonian, Washington DC.

Table of Contents

Poets' Corner

THE SCARF

Marlene Chabot

One end of the chocolate-and-eggshell-blue speckled scarf fluttered in the gentle breeze high above the driver side of a Ford Focus partially raised up over a piece of south lane curbing on Emerson Avenue; the other remained contentedly wrapped around the occupant's delicate cream-colored neck resting on the car's windowsill.

Abigail McPherson stomped on her brakes for the third time in five minutes. *What an evening for a traffic jam.* Everyone was heading out of town to celebrate the Fourth of July, including her.

It took ten more minutes of stops and starts before Abigail's car got within range of what she believed to be the cause of the traffic buildup, a black Ford. Curious, like most other drivers who had passed by already, the woman's gray steely eyes tried to discover what hid behind the thick circle of men in blue buzzing around the Ford. Darn! I can't see the driver, too many cops. But wait. There's loose fabric floating above their heads. A scarf I think. Yes, that's what it is. The driver must be a woman. But what's her problem?

Abigail took a second look at the scarf. It seemed familiar. Too familiar. Nausea swept over her. "No!" She gulped. Her young hands trembled. "It can't be." She inhaled deeply as she stretched out her hand to turn on the Honda's emergency flashers. The car ahead of her noticed her intentions and made space available. Two seconds later

Abigail's car door slammed and she darted to the other side of Emerson Avenue.

She stumbled along drawing ever nearer to the police hovering like mountain lions. Her chest tightened. Could she cope with more bad news today? She didn't think so. Over lunch at work her best friend shared she'd been recently diagnosed with breast cancer. Shocked to the core, twenty-two-year-old Abigail barely managed to squeak out, "Sorry."

A clean-shaven policeman, fresh on the job from Minnesota's Westport Police Academy, tried to deter her from advancing further. "Stop, Miss. I need to see your credentials." She gave him an icy stare. He didn't let up. "Only emergency crew and news reporters are allowed beyond this yellow tape. Are you either of those?"

"No," she stammered, "but I'm concerned about the victim."

Officer Pete Johnson adjusted the visor of his dark-blue cap to shield his eyes from the glaring sun. The woman seemed genuinely upset. He softened. "Sorry, but I'm not allowed to let you go any closer. Tomorrow's paper will have all the details. You'll have to wait till then."

She attempted a feeble smile, remembering politeness is better than a hot temper. "I understand. But couldn't you at least share what happened?"

The newbie cop swiftly digested her request. *What harm could it do?* "A woman was shot."

"Oh my God!" Abigail's eyes jumped beyond the policeman. She saw a snow-white head leaning out the car window with part of the billowing scarf still attached to the neck. "How . . . how badly is she hurt?" When no reply came, a high-pitched wail escaped her quivering lips.

Officer Johnson scanned the crowd. Someone else had to have heard the piercing noise besides him. Hopefully, they wouldn't realize he was partially to blame. He didn't need a complaint filed against him this early in his career.

Focus on the police work, Johnson, he told himself. *You help people no matter what the cost.* He swiftly set aside his concern for his reputation and allowed compassion to take over. He touched Abigail's arm. It felt frail. "Are you all right, Miss?"

Her mouth didn't open.

Sergeant Alice Brandon moved in. She had been keeping close tabs on her department's newest rookie since they arrived on the scene. "Everything okay here, Johnson?"

Johnson stepped aside to make way for his boss. "I... I'm not sure, Ma'am."

Sergeant Brandon studied the badly shaken woman dressed in a two-piece business suit similar in color to the scarf. "What's going on, Miss? We can't help unless you tell us what's troubling you."

Forced to speak despite her mental anguish, Abigail raised her head and said, "Why . . . Why was the woman shot?"

Sergeant Brandon couldn't believe what she heard. She gave the rookie a sharp look before returning her attention to the woman. "What's your name?"

"Abigail McPherson," she stated through tears.

"Do you know the woman in the car?"

"Yes." She pressed a hand against her mouth to control her sobbing. She's my grandmother. Why would someone kill a sweet, elderly woman?"

"I don't know," Sergeant Brandon honestly replied, "but I intend to find out." She hated this part of the job the most, watching people grieve over the death of a loved one and not knowing how to comfort them. "We're looking into the possibility that your grandmother was killed by a stray bullet meant for a rival gang member. There's been a surge of gang-related activity in this part of town over the last two years."

Abigail retrieved a Kleenex from her suit jacket and attempted to wipe her nose. "Last year my father suggested Grandma Ida move closer to us but she adamantly refused. She loved this neighborhood. She said if the neighborhood was good enough to be born in, it was good enough to die in." Abigail sucked in her breath.

"Grandma Ida sounds like one determined woman."

"She was."

Before the middle-aged policewoman could add anything else, the Westport ambulance came to a screeching halt in front of them and paramedics flew into action. A tall female in her early-thirties swung the back of the emergency vehicle open while the forty-year-old-dark-skinned male driver approached Sergeant Brandon. "Did you call this in?"

The sergeant shifted her black, well-worn oxford shoes to get a better view of the emergency medical technician addressing her. She had worked with him before. "Yeah, Chuck," she replied tiredly, wondering when the gang rivalries would end.

"What morgue should we use? St. John's or Fairfax?"

The policewoman decided to let the victim's relative make the decision. "Which hospital is handier for your family, Abigail?"

Abigail looked off in the distance. "I guess Fairfax."

Chuck returned to his partner and helped hoist the gurney on to the ground and over to the Ford. Before opening the left front door to gain access to Ida's body, Jessica gently lifted the elderly woman's small head, removed the long flowing scarf from around her neck, and handed it to Officer Johnson, who had donned rubber gloves.

Johnson placed the scarf in a bag along with all the other non-car related items he had collected. Then the EMT crew lifted the elderly woman's body out of the car and wheeled it back to the ambulance.

Overcome by emotion, Abigail left Sergeant Brandon behind and rushed to the gurney holding her deceased grandmother. "Please, let me say good-bye," she begged.

Brandon nodded her approval.

Officer Johnson finally returned to his supervisor's side and handed off the sealed bag, which she immediately scrutinized. The scarf troubled her. Perhaps the young woman could help. "Abigail."

"Yes?"

"Was your grandmother a follower of Islam?"

4

"A what?"

Brandon repeated herself. "A follower of Islam? A Muslim?"

Abigail frowned. What did Grandmother Ida's beliefs have to do with her death? "Oh?" She thrust her hand towards the bag Sergeant Brandon held. "It's the scarf, the hijab, isn't it?" The policewoman nodded. "It was a gift. Grandma and a neighbor lady, originally from Iraq, became inseparable over the years, almost like sisters. They shared everything: sewing techniques, philosophy on raising children and food preparation."

Brandon couldn't help noticing how Abigail's speaking of her grandmother was taking its toll. "It's a lovely scarf," she remarked soothingly. "Obviously it meant a great deal to her."

"It did."

"Any idea why your grandmother wore it on such an incredibly hot day?"

The young woman's tears disappeared and were replaced by a tiny smile. "Grandma hated air conditioning. It bothered her head." She directed her eyes towards the Focus. "That's why the windows are open. Of course, open windows mess up the hair, and Grandma was a stickler for neatness. Wearing a scarf solved her problem."

The ambulance pulled away and Sergeant Brandon promised to keep the McPherson's informed as the investigation moved forward.

***

Several weeks into the case concerning Ida McPherson's untimely death, small snippets of information began to flow into Sergeant Brandon's police station. The most recent call suggested there was a drug war between two known gangs and the old woman happened to get caught in the crossfire. Even if it was false information, Brandon wasn't ruling it out. Her team would verify the story.

The policewoman looked up from her notes and found Westport's police chief, Gary Hanson, approaching her desk. *What did he have on his mind?* she wondered. "Hello, Chief. What brings you to my turf? If you heard we have donuts to share, that's a myth. No time to stop by the bakery this morning."

Chief Hanson, a heavy-set fellow, didn't find Brandon's comment amusing. The furrows on his thick forehead grew even deeper. "I didn't come here for donuts," he said rather dryly. "I want to know what's happening with the McPherson case. It's been almost a month since her death, and the family is seeking answers."

Picking up on her boss's irritation, Sergeant Brandon calmly replied, "We're making some headway with the leads that have come in, Chief, but no home run yet." She picked up the note lying on her desk and waved it in front of him. "This new bit of information came in five minutes ago."

"Good. Get someone on it, pronto. How about the neighbors? Anyone offered up reliable information yet?"

Sergeant Brandon shook her head. "McPherson was highly respected. No one had anything negative to say." She grabbed another paper. "After retiring from her long teaching career, she offered free tutor services to her neighbors, mostly new immigrants."

Chief Hanson appeared to be appeased by what Brandon had said. He began to step away from her desk. But then bam, his heavy body jerked to a halt, and his mouth slid open. "What about the bullet?"

The sergeant hurriedly dug through the paperwork on her desk again. "According to Wilson, it was a 308."

"Probably came from an M-24 Remington rifle. I can't picture a gang member running around with a piece like that. Can you?"

Brandon swiped the palm of her hand across her desk. "No, Sir."

"Well," the chief said, "I'll leave you to your work then."

6

When Chief Hanson left the confines of Sergeant Brandon's desk behind, Officer Johnson replaced him. "Sergeant."

"Johnson, just the person I wanted to see. I got a call concerning rival gang activity the afternoon Ida McPherson got shot. I want you and Warner to dig a little deeper. Expand your inquiries to the blocks surrounding Emerson Avenue."

"Okay. We'll get right on it. But you might want someone to check out information we received on our tip hotline too."

Brandon tilted her head back slightly. "What have you got?"

"An elderly woman called it in. She lives a block off Emerson, near where we think Ida McPherson was fatally shot. She said she remembers seeing a guy in her alley that day carrying what looked like a rifle over his shoulder. She thought it odd since hunting season isn't for a couple months yet."

"She's the first person to mention a rifle. Do you think she's a believable witness?"

Johnson gazed at the worn oak floor beneath his feet. "She's still working as a seamstress at a very elite dress shop."

"Description?"

The young officer scratched his head searching for a reply.

Brandon tapped her pen on the desk. "I'm waiting Johnson."

"Sorry. I was trying to recall exactly what she said. "A white guy. Mid-fifties. About 5' 11". She said his build's the same as her favorite daytime soap opera character, Tony, a professional golfer."

The policewoman mulled over the information. "Does she drive?"

"No," Johnson hastily reported, "but she said her daughter could bring her tomorrow."

"Before you leave with Warner, call her back. Find out what time she can arrive. I want to have a sketch artist on hand."

"Okay."

"And, Johnson ..."

"Yes?"

"Good job."

"Thanks"

At nine the next morning, a tall, thin woman in her seventies, impeccably dressed in a lime-colored two-piece suit, swept into precinct 29 with a much younger woman following close on her heels. The older woman wasted no time in finding an available policeman to tell him she was here to see Sergeant Brandon.

Officer Stanley grinned. "Name please?"

"Mary Sweeney."

He gazed at the short list of names given to him just moments before, and then he punched in the sergeant's number. "Mary Sweeny is here."

"Please direct her to my desk."

Sergeant Brandon made friendly eye contact with Mary the moment she reached her desk. She wanted to make her feel comfortable. Mary responded accordingly. "Thanks for coming, Ms. Sweeney. We'll try not to keep you too long."

"Thank you. I appreciate that." She quickly glanced at the man already seated by the officer's desk.

Brandon noted her concern and explained as she pointed to an empty chair. "This is Bill, our sketch artist. He's ready to capture everything you say. All we'd like you to do is reply the best you can to his questions concerning the man's features."

As soon as Mary got situated, Bill lifted his drawing materials off his lap and fired questions one after the other. "Pudgy face, long, square? Moles? Any scars? Beard or mustache? Hair style?"

Two hours later, after Mary's departure, Officer Johnson delivered bad news to his boss. "We got zilch, Sarge. The sketch didn't match any mug shots."

"Damn!" Brandon dragged her hand through her short, dark, cropped hair, while staring intently at a copy of Bill's sketch resting on her desk as she did so. The drawing showed a bald-headed man with a high forehead, round face and large cauliflower ears. "Something's got to break," she spouted to no one in particular.

Not knowing if he should take leave, Officer Johnson prattled on. "That older lady has an uncanny memory, doesn't she?"

The policewoman dropped her hand to her side. "Time will tell. All right, Johnson, I need you to fax this picture to the local news station and request it run on tomorrow's news. We've already missed today's deadline."

It turned out posting the picture wasn't necessary after all. That same evening Westport police got their break. A distraught woman called 911 begging for help. "My husband's locked himself in the bathroom and won't come out. Says he's going to kill himself," She sobbed, "I'm afraid he will. He's been hitting the bottle hard these past few weeks and keeps mumbling something about an old woman's death. I haven't a clue what he's referring to."

Sergeant Brandon compared the picture in her hand to the man her fellow officers had just settled in the isolation room. It had to be him. She went over to the nearly-empty coffee machine, filled two cups, and headed towards the room where the man was seated. *Hopefully it's not going to be another long night,* she thought.

Officer Johnson opened the door for his boss. "Thanks," she said, "Call Abigail McPherson. I promised to let her know as soon as we had a suspect in custody."

"Yes, Ma'am."

The door to the isolation room closed quietly behind Sgt. Brandon as she swiftly moved to the table and set the coffee down in front of the suspect.

Lowell Perry greedily drained the two cups of strong coffee in nothing flat.

Hoping the man had settled down a bit after drinking the coffee, she grabbed a chair and sat across from him. "Ready to talk?" she asked, eager to get the interrogation over with.

Perry placed his hands flat on the table and nodded.

Sgt. Brandon leaned in, turned on a tape recorder, and then rested her lanky arms on the table. "Mr. Perry, why did you kill a woman you never met?"

Perry ran his rough hands up and down his distraught face. "I wanted one of them Muslims to suffer like I have, to feel the loss of someone they love."

The policewoman looked at him quizzically. "How have Muslims caused you suffering, sir? None live in your neighborhood."

"Ever since the army notified me of our son's death in Iraq, I haven't been coping well." He braced his forehead with his hands for a moment. "My wife thinks it's depression. I don't know. Maybe she's right. Anyway, a few months back I got this crazy notion if I showed those people what it felt like to lose a loved one, I'd feel better. Except it didn't work. I feel like shit."

Sgt. Brandon felt sorry for the man, but not enough to let a killer off the hook. "Well, Lowell, here's another newsflash. The woman you shot wasn't a foreigner. She was a Westport native."

"But, but she was wearing that scarf."

"The hijab?

"Why would she do that?"

"It was a gift."

Perry Lowell cried, "Oh God!" before his head smacked the table.

THE END

About the Author

Marlene M. Chabot
Marlene Chabot, a native Minnesotan, currently resides in Elk River, Minnesota. She began writing mysteries in 1995. Her freelancing career for magazines, such as *Her Voice,* and other entities in the Central Lakes area took off in 2007. In March 2016 *The Scarf* was selected as a semifinalist in a Neoverse competition.

A member of Sisters in Crime and Marco Island Writers, Marlene received a B.S. degree in education, an A.A.S. business marketing degree and a certificate from the Institute of Children's Literature. Her published writings include five novels— *Detecting the Fatal Connection, North Dakota Neighbor, Mayhem With a Capital M, Death At The Bar X Ranch, Death of the Naked Lady,* and four short stories for anthologies. *A Visit from Santa, The Missing Groom, The Gulper Eel Lounge,* and *Serving Up a Surprise.*

Marlene's novels can be found online at Amazon.com, Barnes and Noble, Createspace and Draft2Digital.
Learn more about this author or her writings at:
www.marlenechabot.com;
marlenechabotbooks.blogspot.com;
Facebook Marlene Mc Neil Chabot

THE THINGS WE DO FOR LUST

Dennis Charles

The Afrika Korpsman rode cautiously into the two-horse town on the southwestern border between Texas and Mexico. It was not quite a border town because that would imply that some nation really governed it. It was late May 1865 and the United States was exhausted by the Civil War and would therefore rarely pay attention to it with units of Union Cavalry. The Mexicans had their own civil war, neither side of which cared at all about this small, not very strategic, village. Local Native American tribes, the Comanche, Navaho and Apache, controlled the mountains, hills, deserts and plains surrounding the town and therefore all access to it. But the people who really controlled this town were the Comancheros, local warlords who traded with Native Americans and a wide range of Mexican and American bandits and mercenaries.

The things we do for lust, the Afrika Korpsman thought, having traveled almost the width of the North American continent and through almost a century and a half in time to find a woman that loved him.

According to any set of conventional wisdom, this woman was no prize. She had a homely but cute face, like a friendly pet rat framed by dull red hair. She had too many freckles on her face and her complexion was overly fair and slightly flawed. Her squinty blue eyes needed glasses or contacts to function properly but that was a minor fix. She was short, five feet one-inches in height, very skinny and flat-chested. Her legs were shapely but skinny and she limped slightly due an injury acquired during the Civil War.

She was also an ex-prostitute and not a very good one at that. Since she was an Irish Catholic, she had said a Hail-Mary after every trick and didn't even finish a second rosary in her years as a camp follower for the Confederacy. She usually worked as a nurse or a teamster driving the hospital wagon or ammunition limbers to pay her way. She had even worked the thirty-two-pounder guns as a powder loader.

She had compassion and practiced the virtue of mercy almost to a fault. She had held his best friend in her arms, talked gently to him and tried to soothe him while he died horribly just before Appomattox.

She could do rudimentary mathematics and knew how to read. On compassion alone, she would make a great doctor someday, if he could only get her back into a DLA/GED program in the twentieth century or use computer based first aid and physicians' assistant training. He could teach her some of the fundamental courses like physics, chemistry, trigonometry and calculus; after all, he was a nuclear physicist. He would go wherever she wanted to, he loved her that much.

But most of all, she loved him. She didn't know about his time-machine and the four hundred million dollars it had earned him in the late twentieth century. She just knew and accepted him, both his gentleness and neuroses.

But now she was missing and he had tracked her here. Train robbers had kidnapped her on the way to St. Louis to get some spectacles. In order to obtain safe passage through the Comanche controlled part of north Texas, they had given her to the Comanche who in turn had traded her to the Comancheros for whisky and weapons.

He had given her a cheap rosary with a tracking device in the oversized crucifix in place of the holy water bottle and told her to keep it with her at all times. It had done its job well. He had followed her here with little or no difficulty. Now the problem was to get her out alive and intact.

When he arrived, he asked for the nearest brothel and was directed to the largest building in town. It was a three-story brown adobe structure with a cantina in the first floor.

He paid a silver dollar to enter the second floor where the prostitutes were and was given a rough wooden token. He examined each of the available small dingy rooms and their occupants. There was a diverse group of women ranging in age from early teens to mid-forties, and belonging to several races, Native American, Mexican and white American.

If a room and woman were in use, a small curtain would be drawn across the doorway to give the customer a vestige of privacy. The curtain did very little to mitigate the sounds however. Groans, grunts and even screams emanated into the corridor.

It was obvious that the women were held against their will. They were chained to the walls or floors of their rooms by metal collars on their ankles, wrists or necks as they sat naked or nearly so on their dirty straw-stuffed mattresses. Most of their expressions were of painful resignation, possibly because they would never leave their little room, at least, alive.

Then he saw the woman he loved. She wasn't even a working prostitute; she was the maid. There was a large metal collar around her neck with a chain long enough for her to go into each of the two-dozen or so rooms. She also had shackles on her knees to prevent her from running. She was collecting a bucket of human waste by emptying bowls of it from the customer-free rooms. She was barefoot and wore the dirty remnant of the light blue slip he had bought for her. Under her right armpit, she carried a bottle of whisky for one of the customers.

Then she saw him. Her squinty eyes widened in fear not joy. She said, "You were right, I shouldn't be a whore. I'm not even good enough for drunken second-rate banditos."

The Afrika Korpsman said, "You're far and away good enough for me. I'm going to get you out of here."

"Get laid and get out. And don't come back. You don't stand a chance against these men," she whispered.

"Who do you recommend?" asked the Afrika Korpsman.

"I can't do you, I'm the maid. Have Sandy do you. She's pretty. She's my friend and needs the tricks. We get paid a slice of bread or a cup beans for every trick. I get scraps. Since there aren't many of those, I'll probably starve in a couple of months. Please don't even think of rescuing me."

Sandy was a pretty, slender but large breasted blonde, who serviced the Afrika Korpsman well. He put the token and a silver dollar in her tip jar. He didn't dare give her a larger one because that might arouse suspicion.

On his way out, since no one was watching, he grabbed the maid and kissed her passionately despite the fact she winced with pain and smelled of sweat, urine and feces. He looked at the back of her slip and saw blood soaking through. "I love you," he said. "I'll be back."

"Please, don't come back. You can't save me."

He spent the next day in the cantina, talking to the townspeople. Thinking he would attempt to offer the owner a price he could not refuse, the Afrika Korpsman wanted to find out two things: 'Who owned the bordello?' and 'What was the going price for these slave-girls?'

About seven in the evening, he met the bordello owner, a huge, tough, bandito warlord, whose shrewdness and

15

casual ruthlessness profoundly scared the Afrika Korpsman who, only a month earlier, had successfully fought against modern, 1990's, Russian mechanized infantry and tanks. No wonder Colleen was afraid for him.

After he bought a second round for the owner, one of the warlord's gunmen came and whispered in his ear. He stood up. "I have business to attend to," he told the Afrika Korpsman. "Justice to mete out and some entertainment to provide."

Following the warlord outside, the Afrika Korpsman found a one-armed ex-Confederate officer, armed with a cap and ball Navy Colt, standing in front of the bandito warlord. The bruises on the ex-officer's face indicated he had been worked over, tilting the playing field in favor of the huge bandito. The bandito warlord berated him for thinking his wife was chained in the bordello. "You're a pitiful cripple. Why shouldn't your wife run away?"

One of the banditos started to count. When he reached three, the warlord and the ex-Confederate officer drew their guns, but the huge bandito was faster and very accurate. He shot the officer in the kneecaps while the one-armed ex-Confederate officer got off a single wild shot as he collapsed. One of the banditos took his pistol and belt from him, rejoicing and waving his new-found treasures.

It took the poor, one-armed ex-Confederate officer an hour to die in absolute agony. If you are at all human and have been in a war, you know that the cries of the dying will haunt your nightmares for many years. Victory better be worth it.

Meanwhile, behind him, the wife of the officer was screaming and cursing the banditos out of the window of her room. Two of the banditos rushed up the stairs and there was the sound of a struggle and several high-pitched screams and then just sobbing.

The two banditos reported back to their leader, who said, "I hope you didn't kill her. If she's dead, the ugly maid will have to use that room."

Later that evening, the Afrika Korpsman returned to the bordello. When he saw his love, Colleen, the maid, he asked for her recommendation. She pointed to an open room, five doors down. The Afrika Korpsman looked to see if anyone could see them and handed her five Power-Protein Energy bars. One of the nearby prostitutes started to scream in Spanish, as he told Colleen, "These things taste terrible, but they're very nutritious. Two of them will feed you for a day. Hang in there. I apologize for using the other girls."

She looked around, and seeing no one in the hall, kissed him. Tears streamed from her squinty, little, but to him beautiful, eyes. She held his hand gently as she led him to the door of the recommended room.

The Afrika Korpsman had gone back to the bordello for a number of reasons. Firstly, he wanted to see the woman he loved and possibly slip her some food and encouragement. Secondly, he wanted to give the impression that he liked the place, so that when he made an offer to buy it or its slaves, the offer would be believable. Finally, he wanted to 'case the joint' in case he had to steal her from her masters.

He looked into the room and saw a slim Native American woman who could have been any age from fourteen to a fit forty. She had a beautiful tan complexion, nice legs and abs and long black hair that was soaked with her own sweat. Her left wrist was nailed to the floorboards with two huge spikes. The wounds in her wrists were getting infected and she was running a fever that coated her body with perspiration. Not only that, her tips jar and food bowl were both empty.

He ran through the curtain and accosted the maid. "Get me a bottle of whisky, and three glasses. Tell them I'm going to do some pre-sex drinking and that you're invited. Get me some water 'cos I'm a wimp."

The maid said, "She somehow got out of her shackles and tried to escape. The bastards nailed her to the floor."

He gave the prostitute a few shots of whisky to kill the pain. He then mixed the whisky and the water and cleansed her wounds. He told the maid, "Have a few drinks, you can use the calories and I need to borrow one of your candy bars."

He gently fed the Power-Protein Energy bar to the sick woman and washed it down with diluted whisky. He then rummaged through his multi-day pill case, mumbling, "Lithium, Prozac, Viagra, Tums, ah, this is what I want— antibiotics. These pills are all supposed to be taken with food."

He looked up at the maid. "I told you I could teach you to be a doctor."

She smiled gently and lovingly at him. Then she heard a sound and looked out the door. "Quickly, get your clothes off," she said. "If she doesn't service you, we're all in trouble. They'll know. The scrawny runt with the shotgun at the back door smells your pants as you leave." She looked around outside again, looked back at him and said, "I love you no matter what."

He administered the pills to the Native American woman. then undressed rapidly. Since she could barely speak English she used gestures to determine the orifice to be used. He was very gentle with her, and despite the context, enjoyed her body. When he was finished, he wiped the sweat off her prostate body with his t-shirt and got dressed. He dropped the token and a silver dollar in her tip jar, hoping that would buy her enough food to keep her alive until he could get her out. As he bent over to pick up his shirt, the Native American woman reached up and gently dragged his face down to hers and kissed him. She murmured two syllables which he didn't understand.

The nuclear physicist was a member of the Fourth Reich and the Students for Separatism and he was dressed like a World War II German soldier, a member of the Deutches Afrika Korps. But he was a political soldier not a mass murderer or slave holder. For this reason, freeing only the woman he loved, Colleen, became morally repugnant. He would have to free all the women in the bordello not just her.

The next day he found the owner and he started to discuss business with him. He had counted two dozen rooms of which about five were empty. This meant the bordello probably employed twenty slaves and the maid. Since he had read that in the south, before the Civil War, good slaves cost $2000 apiece, he reasoned that a good offer would be:

$40,000 slaves

$10,000 building

$5,000 closing cost

$20,000 bandito severance pay

$25,000 franchise rights

$100,000 Total

—a chunk of change in the mid-19th century.

However, the 4th Reich was worth several billion dollars in the late twentieth century and had stashed away large amounts of money in the form of gold bullion. This money was to be used to finance its operations in the Civil War, buy freedom for as many slaves as possible, buy food and medicine for Civil War refugees and pay for trips to New Orleans to visit the classy Story Town bordellos. After all, the scientists and engineers in the 4th Reich were socially dysfunctional nerds who couldn't get a date for the prom with a girl on the chess team even if they themselves were on the chess team.

There was a well-concealed stash of 250 five-pound gold bars within twenty miles of the village. This money was to be used to help Maximilian III hire mercenaries from the shattered Union Army. However, since the 4th Reich's operations in the Civil War had failed, this money would be wasted on Maximilian III's dubious cause because if the Confederacy lost, so would Maximilian III, at least, in the long run. The French and later the Germans would be denied their colony in North America.

The Afrika Korpsman started his bidding at $25,000. The giant rejected it and said to come back with a better offer the following day.

The Afrika Korpsman went to the bordello that night and gave the maid a small package containing a dozen Power-Protein Energy bars, her small derringer with a dozen extra bullets and some antibiotics for the injured Native American woman. It also contained a book of matches and a plastic bag full of little metallic strips. When the moaning was loud enough in the corridor to cover his voice, he explained the contents of the package. "I got you some more candy bars. Don't share them. Keep your strength up. You're going to need it. I'm going to try to buy this place tomorrow. If that doesn't work, you'll have to break out of here yourself."

When the moaning lessened, he said, "Bring me a bottle of whisky and two glasses. And water because I'm a wimp. Tell them I don't like drinking alone."

The maid brought the whisky and two glasses and he asked, "Who do you recommend?" She led him to a room at the other end of the corridor. Inside, was a Hispanic woman with a slim but womanly figure wearing a dirty, torn dress. She had expressive dark eyes and long hair framed her lovely face.

"Her name is Rosita. She's very nice, speaks English and needs the tips."

The moaning with pleasure resumed and he further explained his package to Colleen. "Wrap the little metal strips around your chains and light them. The strips are thermite alloy, a metal that will burn so hot, they'll melt the iron. If I fail to buy this place, you'll have to break out, two days after tomorrow, an hour before sunrise. Here's a map. I'll wait for you. If I'm not there, go without me. I've got you a horse, water and food. I'll find you."

The noise level in the hall decreased and he whispered gently, "I won't leave this town without you. Unless it's feet first."

Rosita removed her dirty dress and he saw her badly damaged back. She had been bullwhipped for refusing one of the gang's pistoleros as a customer. The Afrika Korpsman gave her a few shots of whisky to help kill the pain and then cleaned her wounds with the water and whisky. In return, she entertained him more than competently.

He dressed and walked down the corridor, looking for the maid. When he found her, he looked around furtively and finding no one else visible, kissed her gently. "I love you. We'll be together soon."

The Afrika Korpsman went to the cantina the next day, offering the huge bandito $55,000 for the bordello. The bandito and his gang would get to keep the cantina. That bid was rejected as was the bid of $75,000. This bid at least got the huge bandito interested enough to ask, "In dollars or pesos?"

"Bullion, in five-pound bars," the Afrika Korpsman answered.

"Show me the gold and we talk some more," said the Giant Bandito.

The next day, the Afrika Korpsman brought two gold bars as samples and presented them to the bandito warlord, who said, "Now we know that you have gold. How much do you wish to bid?"

"$100,000."

"I have an idea. You give me the gold and I let you live," said the Warlord.

"I don't have it here. It's buried in the desert," said the Desert Warrior.

"Tell me where it is and I might let you live and give you one of my whores as a going away present."

"No way. Besides none of those whores are worth more than two dollars a trick at the most."

The Afrika Korpsman started to walk away knowing he would probably never free the woman he loved. Tears welled up in his eyes as he stumbled away. Then he heard a shot and saw a small geyser of sand right in front of him. He turned and saw the huge bandito pointing his cap-and-ball revolver at him.

"I am serious about that gold," said the Warlord calmly.

"If you kill me, you'll never find it, not in a million years. You need one of these things." The Afrika Korpsman held up the receiver for the tracking system, which looked like an over-sized cell phone. "I'll fight you for it," he said.

One of the pistoleros walked out to the Afrika Korpsman and offered him a revolver. The Afrika Korpsman rejected it and said, "You use your gun and I'll use mine. I'll fight you tomorrow at four in the afternoon. That'll be after I prepare a map to the gold, which you can take off my dead body if you win. I'll take the whorehouse lock stock and barrel if I win." Thinking he would rather have the entire gang in front of him than spread out and possibly behind him, he said, "I'll give you another little edge; your entire gang can be your second."

"One of my men will stay with you tonight to make sure you draw the map and don't run away," said the huge bandito.

"OK, as long as he doesn't bring a gun with him."

Julio, give me your gun and go with him," said the Warlord. Julio dutifully gave the huge bandito his pistol belt and followed the Afrika Korpsman to his suite of hotel rooms.

That night, the Afrika Korpsman assembled his weapons. First, he assembled his primary weapon, his reliable and accurate MG34, the standard light machinegun of Germany during World War II that fires 1200 rounds per minute and has an effective range of over 2000 yards. It was virtually identical to the M60 light machine except for the longer barrel, slightly different layout and better sights, especially for long range. The Afrika Korpsman had used the MG34 against the Russians in Northern Virginia and trained real soldiers to use the M60 during the Vietnam War.

On seeing the MG34, Julio said, "That's a mighty big gun."

The Afrika Korpsman replied, "Your warlord is a mighty big man. I'm going to test fire it."

He inserted a single bullet into the breech and fired his machinegun out the window. Julio smiled at the single shot, probably thinking the MG34 was a glorified single shot rifle. The Afrika Korpsman ran a rod down the barrel and squirted some white liquid in the breech.

He then programmed the tracker to lead the banditos to a storehouse containing high explosives, about fifty miles from the village. Furthermore, the storehouse was booby trapped. If the wrong access code was used, a ton of high explosives would destroy everything within a two-hundred-yard radius. The banditos would lose even if they won.

As backup, the Afrika Korpsman armed himself with a NP-40 machine pistol and a Luger pistol. He was familiar with both weapons but hardly an expert. He would use them only if the MG34 jammed or ran out of ammunition, which was highly unlikely since he would be carrying over 500 rounds.

At 4 P.M., all was ready and the Afrika Korpsman dressed for the final showdown. He said to Julio, "Please, hand me my vest."

"Which one?"

"The one marked K-E-V-L-A-R," said the Afrika Korpsman.

Armed and armored, the Afrika Korpsman walked slowly toward the cantina. In front of him were a dozen banditos armed with various types of revolvers. Despite the distinct advantage in firepower and the bullet-proof vest, shear weight of numbers would probably prevail. Besides, the warlord would probably shoot him in the knees where there was no Kevlar protection.

To avoid bloodshed, including his own, the Afrika Korpsman tried to make a deal. "I'll give you $150,000 in gold for the women alone."

"No deal, we fight," said the Warlord.

"You guys don't understand. This weapon is very powerful. It fires 1200 rounds a minute just like 200 revolvers. And at this range I'm not going to miss," said the Afrika Korpsman. He was standing forty yards away from the Warlord, barely within pistol range. He started backing away slowly so he would be out of effective pistol range when the time came.

Julio, who was now standing next to the Warlord, said, "It only fires one shot, he's bluffing."

The Afrika Korpsman, backing away slowly, was now fifty yards from the Warlord when he heard the words, "Draw on three, ready," and the count started.

However, the pistoleros on the far end drew on two. A round hit Afrika Korpsman in the chest knocking him down but not hurting him. He opened fire from the prone position. A short burst killed the two of them and sent the others running for cover inside the cantina.

The Warlord drew his weapon and fired. He was a master gunfighter comparable to Billy the Kid, Wild Bill Hickok or John Wesley Hardin. But while he was a master of the Colt revolver, his opponent was a master of the MG34 light machinegun. Furthermore, the Warlord was used to fighting men who were either totally inferior to him or softened up a bit by his gang. The Afrika Korpsman had both trained and fought against real soldiers. The outcome of their duel was almost a foregone conclusion, reached when a burst from the MG34 almost tore the Warlord in half.

Julio was very brave but even more incompetent. Firing his pistol wildly, he charged the machine gunner. When he got to within fifteen yards, he ran out of ammunition. The Afrika Korpsman gave him a chance to throw down his gun but he chose to reload instead. "Idiot!" said the Afrika Korpsman, dispatching Julio with a single head-shot.

The pants-smeller fired his shotgun at the Afrika Korpsman. The pellets simply bounced off the bullet proof plastic faceplate attached to the Afrika Korpsman's World War II German helmet. The pants-smeller was reaching for his revolver when he was hit by a short burst from the machinegun.

Four of the Warlord's gang ran upstairs into the brothel. As one of them drew a bead on the Afrika Korpsman with his musket, the maid shot him with her derringer. Then she rushed down the hall while reloading her tiny weapon and shot a very clueless bandito standing in the hall, reloading.

The third bandito made the mistake of setting up in Sandra's room. Sandra wrapped her chain around his neck and strangled him. When she was finished, she looked at her chains and said, "I knew they were good for something."

The fourth bandito went to Rosita's room and took careful aim at the Afrika Korpsman. However, since he never said, "may I" to the occupant she belted him with her chamber pot. Rosita and the bandito were struggling desperately when the maid came in and shot him twice with her derringer.

Three more banditos still lurked inside the cantina. The Afrika Korpsman offered to let them surrender by throwing their guns out. They refused, possibly assuming they would get the warlord's territory and money if they could kill the Afrika Korpsman.

The Afrika Korpsman switched the belt in his weapon from ball to armor piercing. One of the remaining banditos fired a few rounds at the Desert Warrior and he replied with the armor piercing bullets, which shredded the adobe walls of the cantina and wounded the bandito in the leg. His screaming echoed through the cantina and probably demoralized the other banditos. They decided to run and made easy targets on horseback even over a half a mile away. The wounded man was put out of his misery by one of the other banditos.

After the battle, Colleen and the Afrika Korpsman spent hours freeing and helping the women. He got them baths, clothes and bought them meals at the hotel with his gold. He provided as much first aid as possible within the limitations of his National Guard training, three hours a year, and meager resources, about 90 aspirins and 20 cheap generic antibiotics.

The Afrika Korpsman did his best to send the women back home. He used his gold to buy them clothes, food and either horses or stage transport and provided each of them with $100 traveling money. However, a number of the women had nowhere to go, no families and no skills except prostitution.

One of them was Sandra who asked Colleen, "Where did you get a great guy like him? I'd like one."

The Afrika Korpsman overheard them and had an idea.

June 2005, The United States

The nuclear physicist, wearing his dark blue suit, sat proudly in the Auditorium of Tesla Community College. Next to him sat the experimental physicist with his young wife. Since the graduation was taking place before a semi-formal gala, the experimental physicist's wife, Patricia, wore a black evening gown that showed off her excellent legs, slender figure and beautiful tan skin. The only flaws in her appearance were two large scars on her left wrist. It was obvious from her expression that she was very happy with the experimental physicist.

The mechanical engineer's wife, Sandra, was also stunning in a low-cut white evening gown that complemented her slender but voluptuous figure. Her affectionate manner before the start of the proceedings showed that she was also deeply in love with her spouse.

Rosita looked beautiful in her royal blue evening gown. She gazed at the Computer Scientist with love in her eyes. Their adopted 12-year-old daughter, also from the bordello, was pretty, happy and healthy.

Finally, a small, skinny, red-haired woman limped onto the stage and accepted her diploma. The technocrats and their wives cheered loudly. The red-haired woman smiled and waved her diploma at them in response. The nuclear physicist looked at her with both pride and love in his eyes. You would think that she was a beautiful actress that was getting an Oscar or Emmy not a limping, scrawny, homely, ex-prostitute getting her Associates Degree in Nursing.

It was the first graduation for the wives of the members of the 4th Reich. However, it would certainly not be the last.

Sandra had finished her first year in general studies. She wanted to go to a real college. Patricia, originally Cautious Deer, was taking GED preparation courses, introduction to computers and ESOL, English as a Second Language. For fun, Rosita, was also taking ESOL, World Literature I, and pre-college mathematics classes as well. The technocrats wanted their wives to have an education so they could be more independent. The nerds wanted to be loved but not by default.

All the new spouses for the technocrats of the 4th Reich were very enamored of their husbands. After all, they had gone from starving prostitute-slaves to the semi-trophy wives of multimillionaires. They had been given extensive medical treatments including those for social diseases, round worm infestation, malnutrition, dehydration and physical trauma. A little nipping and tucking, Botox and silicon were fitted into the treatment schedule and converted the slightly better than average looking slaves into good approximations of trophy wives.

The nerdy technocrats of the 4th Reich were used to treating women politely and decently, otherwise they would never get a date. A little kindness was all it took to make these nerds as attractive as Fabio. The new wives were quite simply treated like princesses. A few pheromones didn't hurt either.

These were matches made in heaven or at least a very benign wormhole.

THE END

ALL IS FAIR IN LOVE, WAR AND ROLLER DERBY

Dennis Charles

The University of Chicago, May 10, 1970

The time traveling operative easily found the radical socialist campus leader, a very important person in that he was the coordinator of the radical student movement throughout the Midwest of the United States.

The leaders of the radical movement considered the Midwest to be pivotal in the initiation of 'The Revolution' simply because student leaders assumed they could take over the Northeast and the West Coast quite easily. The South would probably not fall to the new left but would have to be subjugated by force later. Thus, the fate of the Midwest was of primary importance, and for these reasons, this campus leader was given the authority to start the series of confrontations and demonstrations that would initiate 'The Revolution'.

Due to the utterance of a prearranged password, the student leader thought that the time traveling operative was a fellow leftist graduate student and took an immediate liking to him and told him of their plans for 'The Revolution'. The student leader told the operative, "We can't lose. We've war gamed it. The fascist pigs don't stand a chance. Power to the people!"

"Did anyone represent the fascists?" asked the operative.

"Yes, one of the members of the SDS, a young and ardent socialist."

"No wonder you won, the socialist probably threw the game," the time traveling operative said.

"We're going to play tomorrow afternoon, and after the game we're gonna party. I've got lots of grass but you're gonna have to bring your own beer and some munchies," said the student leader.

"You should invite a real fascist pig to play and then you can determine whether 'The Revolution' is really feasible or not. This'll also give you a chance to refine your strategy," said the time traveling operative. They were going to war game Saturday afternoon and party Saturday night. *When do they study?'* he wondered.

"Yeah, but this is the University of Chicago, where are we going to find a real fascist?" asked the radical student leader.

The time traveling operative thought *if you get into power all you'll have to do is look in the mirror.* Then remembering his duty, the operative said, "I know one, he's almost ideal."

The student eyed the operative with interest. "Really?"

"Really—he's a member of the National Guard, a Young Republican, a physics major and a real nerd. He'll do his damnedest to beat you and you'll enjoy beating him and the establishment."

***

Saturday Afternoon in the University of Chicago
Student Union Ping-Pong Room

A large collection of student radicals sporting beards, long hair or Afros and wearing T-shirts emblazoned with various leftist political slogans and symbols, gathered around the three ping-pong tables. The ping-pong tables had been stripped of their nets and were covered with maps. These maps represented a number of large Midwestern cities and were over-laid with hexes, just like Avalon-Hill war games.

The fascist pig was a slender young man dressed in slacks and a short-sleeved shirt. In this attire that today would be referred to as business casual, he looked out of place. Furthermore, his glasses and demeanor made him appear really nerdy.

He felt really nerdy as well. Wednesday, he had asked Diane out for Saturday night and she had accepted. She had called him Friday night and cancelled. Now he knew why. She was currently sharing a badly used joint with the student leader. She probably had decided to go out with the student leader instead of him. She was the nerd's 'Rocks and Stars', General Science 102 lab partner and a good friend. He had been hoping for maybe more.

She looked his way and smiled sheepishly. The student leader smirked, walked over to him and said, "All's fair in love." Then he walked back to Diane, put his hands on her lower back and slid them downward slowly. Diane reacted with another weak smile and then sucked deeply on the joint.

The nerd really disliked the radical student's smugness, especially since he had the pick of the campus women, which included coeds, secretaries and even young female professors. In the late 60s and the early 70s, campus radical leaders had replaced star football players and big men on campus as status dates. Because she was too thin, somewhat

31

flat-chested and cute rather than pretty, the student leader would probably soon find greener pastures with someone else. If you don't believe that liberals are status seekers, ask yourself why BMW is still in business.

There and then pathetic nerd/fascist resolved to defeat the radicals whatever it took.

But he certainly didn't act that way especially early in the war game: he reacted poorly to their moves using his 'Cops' pieces rather haphazardly against their 'SDS', and 'Black Power' pieces. The 'Jane Fonda' piece was then used and the fascists/conservatives were really on the run.

The fact that he was very badly outnumbered didn't help. He was the only fascist there and had to work all three game boards at the same time. The radicals had at least two players per board as well as the student radical leader as coordinator. From their beards and t-shirts, although covered up by striped basketball referee shirts, it was obvious the referees were very sympathetic to the cause of the radicals.

However, he got the upper hand when he used his 'FBI' pieces against them. The radicals countered with the 'William Kunstler' and 'Radical Lawyer' pieces and the biggest piece so far in the game: the 'Constitution' piece.

These three sets of cardboard markers almost completely trumped the 'FBI' pieces and kept the nerd from removing all but two of his captured pieces from the board.

He countered with his 'Redneck' and 'Labor Union' pieces. The communist protested that the 'Labor Union' pieces were on the side of the radicals not the pigs. The referee conceded that their loyalty to either side was at best ambiguous and it was decided that neither side could use them.

All the while the fascist was moving his 'NG' pieces to hexes near the outskirts of the cities and during that time he was also cutting a piece of cardboard into game pieces and writing something on them.

The radical socialists tried to start a general strike. However, the fascist objected. One of the referees decreed that the 'Labor Union' pieces were necessary for that to happen and they had been removed from the game.

***

The 'Student' pieces were then used and several 'Bomb' pieces were placed in significant locations like the Commodities Exchange and several science buildings which possibly had Defense contracts of some sort. Some of the 'Black Power' pieces were brought into play to eliminate a number of 'Cop' and 'FBI' pieces. On the next move, two of the cities were on the verge of falling to the radicals. According to the board game, capitalism was now on the run, it was only a matter of time.

The moment was right for the fascist to make his move and it was a dilly. He placed cardboard markers with poorly drawn mushroom clouds and labeled '1/2 KT', '1 KT' and '2 KT' on both college campuses and minority areas including public housing projects and slums in the seven Midwestern cities.

"What's that?" asked the Black Panther.

"Low yield tactical nuclear warheads," said the fascist.

"Where do they come from?" asked one of the referees.

"From these National Guard nuclear artillery units," answered the fascist pointing to several 'NG' markers near each city.

"Won't nuclear weapons destroy the cities?" asked a member of the SDS.

"These weapons have very small yields that have been adjusted to the size of their targets. They'll probably just destroy the colleges and the projects. Most parts of the cities with their factories, commercial centers and financial district would likely remain intact except for a little fallout—maybe.

The suburbs won't be touched," added the fascist.

"That's impossible! You don't know what you're talking about," stated another radical socialist.

"I ought to know, I'm the assistant weaponeer in the 1st Illinois Nuclear Artillery," said the fascist.

"That's mass murder, a war crime!" screamed one of the Weatherman, an extremely violent branch of the SDS.

"Terrorism is also against international law," countered the fascist.

The fascist now realized that he was scaring the crap out of these commie-type hippy fags—good. The time traveling operative concealed his smile because he shared the sentiments of the pathetic nerd but didn't want to alienate the radicals, he had to manipulate them.

"I'm gonna ask for immediate Soviet and Chinese military intervention," yelled one of the radicals.

The communist emptied a plastic bag containing dozens of cardboard markers representing Soviet Army units next to the map of Cleveland.

"You can't do that, this is a civil war. You've applied that criterion to the Vietnam War thereby deeming it immoral. You have to apply it to this situation as well. Foreign intervention is out," said the nerd.

"All's fair in love and war," added the radical student leader.

"You've got two other problems—The Atlantic and Pacific Oceans. The Russian Navy has to defeat the U.S. Navy to land troops in the U.S. and that's not going to be easy," continued the nerd/fascist.

The communist bristled. "Of course, it will be easy."

The time traveling operative added, "The United States Navy with its aircraft carriers, nuclear submarines and huge fleet of destroyers would easily defeat the Russian Navy despite its twenty-five heavy cruisers and vast fleet of diesel powered submarines. These old diesel-powered subs are both very slow and very short ranged. The Russians have few nuclear subs and these are both slower and noisier than their American counterparts. A landing of the Soviet Army on American soil, except for possibly Alaska, would be virtually impossible."

"Isn't the morale of the fascist American Navy very low? Won't they surrender to just about anyone?" asked a socialist.

"I know about morale in the Navy; I was discharged just last year. It's not that low. Remember the crews are all volunteers not draftees," said the time traveling operative.

The communist called a time-out which was granted by the referees. During this short respite, the time traveling operative told the pathetic nerd, the referees and a few of the radicals about the 1917 French Army mutinies where the infantry refused to attack the Germans but held the line against them and later won the war in 1918. This further bolstered his case for the near impossibility of a Soviet invasion.

The communist then played his trump pieces on all seven cities. The pieces were labeled 'ICBM-100 MT'. He screamed, "Take that, you damned fascist pigs!"

With the total annihilation of the United States and possibly the world, the referees ended the game and declared it a draw. Besides it was almost five in the afternoon, and they wanted to start partying.

The time traveling operative snickered because this result was exactly what Santa and his Elves had predicted. Fortunately, it was with cardboard markers not real ICBM's and radical students playing a board game not world leaders trying preserve the peace or at least the status quo.

After the game, the time traveling operative joined the radical students partying. About eight o'clock, the beer, pot and munchies started to run out and the radicals began to get bored. The time traveling operative pulled out seven tickets to, of all things, Roller Derby and talked the radicals into going.

The radicals enjoyed the Roller Derby match between the Chicago Pioneers and the California Invaders since the competition was fierce, funny and a bit chaotic. Being somewhat drunk and really stoned didn't hurt much either. They marveled at the chaos on the track and summed it up with the statement: 'All's fair in Roller Derby'.

After making love with Diane, the student leader left his bed rather disappointed at the sex. Diane was not pretty enough and she was too small and thin for his taste. Furthermore, her technique was not up to par even for a freshman and she was not quite as adventurous as he would have liked. He set the alarm clock ahead two hours. He would wake her up and she would provide him with some more low-quality sex, which is certainly better than none at all. He certainly wouldn't date her again, he could do better from the other campus women.

Being slightly wired, the student leader looked for something to read. He found the two books left by his new friend. He started reading the first, *The First World War*, at its inserted bookmark, which described the conditions in Russia in 1917, just before the revolution. In both America in 1970 and Russia in 1917, the country was losing a war and both countries were ethnically diverse. However, that was where the analogy ended. Russia had lost over three million men in World War I, America only around fifty thousand in Vietnam. German troops occupied huge stretches of Russia, the NVA didn't have a single soldier on the North American continent. Furthermore, in Russia in 1917, the average person was starving and freezing due to war-time shortages and destitute economy; America in 1970 had far and away the highest standard of living in the world.

What made him shudder was that the revolution to end the war, World War I, only served to ignite the Russian civil war where Russia had between four and ten million dead, several wars along the coast of the Baltic and the Russo-Polish war of the early 1920's where the casualties weren't even counted. If the southern United States didn't succumb to the radicals easily, then such an internecine civil war might easily occur and, thanks to the efficiency of modern warfare technology, generate tens of millions of casualties.

While at Roller Derby, the radicals marveled at what they called the 'real-world people', their term for the working-class and middle-class Americans watching the game. A number of them mentioned the profound differences between the academics and the 'real-world people.' Maybe the 'Labor Union' pieces did indeed belong to the fascists. That was probably true for the 'Suburbanite' pieces as well.

What about the 'VFW' pieces? The radical leader had seen too many 'If you love your freedom, thank a vet' bumper stickers in the stadium parking lot.

Furthermore, there was an epidemic of those stupid American flag decals all over the cars in the stadium parking lot and on the walls and even the subway. What did that mean?

He then read the second book, *The Road between the Wars,* starting at its bookmark. The bookmarked pages described in detail the burning of the Reichstag and how it converted Hitler from the President and Chancellor of the Weimar Republic into the extremely popular dictator of the 3rd Reich.

After having sex with the willing but scrawny, unattractive and incompetent Diane for the third time at ten in the morning, he called the national coordinator and told him that he could not deliver the Midwest and that he thought that 'The Revolution' was fraught with extreme peril. The national coordinator decided to postpone 'The Revolution' and work within the system at least for the time being.

THE END

The Plea

Dennis Charles

It was obvious from the demeanor of the prisoner that he despised, at the very least, his captors. The prisoner looked extremely tough. He was clad in his expensive Miami-style casual clothes, which revealed his huge steroid-bloated muscles. His arms and neck were festooned with gangland tattoos and a bandana showing his gang allegiance was perched atop his shaved head. He even blew the smoke from his ten-dollar Cuban cigar at the face of the nearest of his captors causing him to blink.

His captors, however, were four somewhat nondescript, slightly built men, one of which didn't even have two good arms. They were too nerdy-looking to even be cops.

Willie, spoke first. "Do we have a deal for you. All you have to do is tell us everything you know about the activities of the Los Bandidos gang, and we'll forget about any charges."

"You've got nothing to hold me on," said the prisoner.

"Oh, yes we do," replied a tall but nerdy looking man, who was both a theoretical nuclear physicist and a near expert with computers. Besides programming in seven different languages, the tall nerd was also adept at firewall penetration and computer file decryption.

The prisoner was both a murderer and drug dealer among other things. For those reasons, he did indeed have something to hide.

"We have lots of evidence: photographs, tape recordings, e-mails, offshore bank transactions, plus a detailed audit of your recent cash transactions. The IRS might want to know about that," added the nuclear physicist.

The nuclear physicist also had pictures of the drug dealer at the clothing optional beach. The drug dealer often went there to pick up women—he liked to see the entire package before he made his move. He was also very proud of his muscular build, body art and the fact that he was well endowed and circumcised.

The nuclear physicist's skinny, plain and almost equally nerdy-looking wife had taken these pictures. One of her more attractive friends had helped her by preying on the vanity of the macho he-man.

The drug dealer's tattoos commemorated his numerous gang exploits including at least seven murders. These tattoos were quite easy to interpret. A murder was symbolized by a small stick figure with an appropriate prop. A popsicle was the prop used to denote the murdered ice cream man. Sandra's stick figure was right next to that of the ice cream man and had a huge shock of yellow hair. The nuclear physicist duly noted that less than half of the victims had a gang logo or weapon associated with them.

Multi-million-dollar drug shipments were denoted by the mode of transport, tiny pictures of boats, airplanes and trucks. Sometimes, even the drug of choice, cocaine or heroin, was described. Acts of extortion were symbolized by shattered panes of glass. The drug dealer's body was literally covered with these semi-obscenities—he had been a very naughty boy.

However, none of this evidence or its interpretation was acceptable in court and the four nerds knew it. It was apparent that the drug dealer also knew that when he asked for his lawyer. However, the four nerds were vigilantes not cops and they wanted revenge not just sham justice.

"You're a very big fish, but we want the sharks if possible. Maybe even one of the whales," added the particle physicist.

"Hopefully, Moby Dick," said Willie.

It was obvious from the perplexed expression on the drug dealer's face that he hadn't read Herman Melville or even watched many movies.

"We don't want information about your present gang. We want you to talk about Los Bandidos, your old gang. I take it from your body art that the parting was not cordial," added the nuclear physicist.

"You can consider it payback," said the particle physicist. Payback was what he wanted—the drug dealer had murdered Sandra, his beautiful, loving, sexy wife.

"I'm not a rat, and I want my lawyer," reiterated the drug dealer.

"We didn't detain you to put you in jail. All we want is information," said the nuclear physicist.

"In fact, I have a plan whereby this information can benefit us both," added Willie.

"How so?" asked the drug dealer.

"If we put Los Bandidos out of business, L-18 will prosper. If we then gut the middle management of L-18, you could emerge as a very big shark in a nearly empty ocean," said Willie.

"You won't have to testify in court. All you have to do is point us in the right direction," said the fourth captor, a paralegal who had been an engineer. Being displaced from his aerospace job, he had gone to a junior college and then obtained a federally funded internship with the Los Angeles District Attorney. While visiting his mother in Florida, he had visited his old friends and co-workers and they had asked a favor of him.

"I won't rat out my friends," insisted the drug dealer.

"You're not going to rat out your friends. You're going to betray your enemies. Probably just before they betray you," said the particle physicist.

"I'm a federal prosecutor, so I have a great deal of leeway in this negotiation. Let's make it even more worth your while. I am prepared to give you full immunity for all of your crimes, if you cooperate," said the paralegal, stretching the truth. He was an assistant to a federal prosecutor and he had been allowed to fine tune a number of plea bargains. He had been allowed to negotiate the federal facility and sometimes even the terms of probation for some of these pleas.

"A large crowd saw him resist arrest. We can't just let that go away or the two gangs will smell something," said Willie.

"What if I offer you concurrent sentences for all of your indiscretions in return for the necessary information?" asked the paralegal.

The drug dealer showed interest. "How long a sentence?"

"Three to six months. However, we will choose the institution. As a bonus, so you won't feel like a rat, I'll even ask you for a list of your friends whom we won't prosecute, at least in the near future," said the paralegal.

"I want my lawyer to read the papers."

"That would be really stupid," said the paralegal.

"Why?"

"Because he's not your lawyer, he's L-18's lawyer. Who do you think pays his retainer?" asked the paralegal.

"We know of a nice co-ed facility we can get to in less than an hour. Neither Los Bandidos nor L-18 can get to you there. You'll be safe from them there."

"There aren't any concrete walls around it. Kind of like a country club for white collar criminals," added the paralegal.

"We'll even agree not to touch any of your ill-gotten gains. Your assets of every kind won't be confiscated for any reason even as evidence against the other gang members," said the nuclear physicist. "We'll even give you some traveling money to help buy you some sundries in prison."

"How much?" asked the drug dealer.

"Maybe a few thousand, depends on what kind of information you give us," said the nuclear physicist.

"I think there's an ATM in the facility," added Willie.

The drug dealer closed his eyes and a small smile flickered across his face. From his expression, the four nerds knew exactly what he was thinking, that he could easily dominate the embezzlers and other white-collar wimps and the fact that the prison was co-ed meant he could have all the women he needed, all he had to do was pay or persuade them.

After about a minute, the drug dealer opened his eyes and nodded agreement. He signed the paper giving him a preliminary form of immunity and listed his good friends in both organizations and had the nuclear physicist sign the agreement to not prosecute them for at least one year.

Then the drug dealer spent almost two hours describing the operations and hierarchies of the two gangs, implicating several members of Los Bandidos and L-18 in murders and hijacking. He even told the nerds where both gangs stored their drugs and guns and bought their other supplies. He answered the questions about money laundering in detail naming several banks and real estate agents. He answered all the questions put to him without a hint of evasion or arrogance. He even drew a number of detailed maps and floor plans and provided e-mail addresses and web sites of the L-18 drug middlemen.

Then he confessed to nine murders, including that of Sandra, numerous other violent crimes and a vast array of drug related offenses. He finished his confession by signing the plea agreement making all these crimes concurrent with the resisting arrest charge and limiting his jail time to no more than six months and no less than three.

In less than an hour the drug dealer and three of the nerds were flying north over the Gulf of Mexico. The nuclear physicist looked back at the drug dealer and said, "He's asleep."

"That's not surprising, guilty men sleep very well in prison while the innocent have insomnia," said Willie.

"That'll make this somewhat easier," said the particle physicist who was piloting the small seaplane. He pushed a red button on the dash board and a glowing orange and purple circle appeared in front of the small seaplane. He deftly pointed the small aircraft into the center of the circle.

When they exited from the glowing circle, the green of the Gulf of Mexico was converted to the gray of the Baltic.

The nerds were adept time-travelers and they had traveled in four dimensions to an earlier era in north central Europe.

When they landed, they were greeted by a man in a fancy black uniform who greeted them with a hearty, "*Heil Hitler.*"

The particle physicist returned the greeting in German, "*Heil Hitler* to you. We have a customer for you. He's a little tired. I think he needs a shower."

The nerds had been true to their word, the facility did not have concrete walls, was indeed co-ed and was not associated with Dade county or the state of Florida. It was Auschwitz, a World War II Nazi death camp.

THE END

Ben His (Private)

Dennis Charles

The bank faced a major problem; Donald Clubs, the mercurial entrepreneur, had recently declared bankruptcy. He owed the bank well over two billion dollars. But the bank would have to wait in line with several other creditors to whom he owed considerably over five billion dollars.

The Banker said, "Clubs has got the money somewhere. This is his third bankruptcy and he always recovers from each of them quickly and easily. They don't even affect his lifestyle. He's still escorting actress/models and eating lobster while his creditors' employees are collecting unemployment insurance."

"He's the master of the deal. That's he how wriggles out," commented the Senior Vice President.

"There are other masters in this universe," said the Banker.

"John Maynard Keynes, the Master of Economics is one of them and he says, "'If you owe your banker a thousand pounds, he owns you. If you owe your banker a million pounds, you own him,'" quoted the Junior Vice President.

They called Donald Clubs to the meeting. He was dressed neatly in dark gray business suit with matching vest, a yellow silk shirt and, of course, a red power tie. He acted with assurance if not arrogance, as if the bankers owed him the money not the other way around.

One of the Vice Presidents almost immediately signaled the Banker that Donald had recently indulged himself in some designer drugs. The proper mixture of these mood-elevating drugs would facilitate Donald's negotiation, making him feel invulnerable and readily able to bully his opponent into making ill-advised concessions.

The Banker introduced Donald to the directors of the bank. They chatted pleasantly and then swapped golf stories, fishing stories and mistress stories. The Banker concluded that Donald was a superbly, if not dangerously, charming individual. Finally, the small talk ended and they got down to the business at hand

"You're not doing very well right now, Donald. Your casinos are losing money. The occupancy factors in your high-rise apartments are quite low. In fact, since the rents have also fallen precipitously and since those buildings are mortgaged to the hilt, you are now losing money on residential rental property. That's very hard to do especially in Manhattan," said the Senior Vice President.

"The Clubs Airline is also generating a lot of red ink. However, you have an excuse. None of the other airlines are doing well either. Only two of the twenty major carriers are operating reasonably far in the black. Airline management blames it on 9/11. I blame it on incompetence," said the Junior Vice President.

The Senior Vice President added, "The enrollment in your online university is sagging as are the ratings of two television shows 'The Journeyman' and 'Clubs Corner.'

Little wonder. Your stock predictions have been absolutely awful."

"You're even losing money on "Clubs—The Game," said The Banker.

Donald stared at him, mute but nonplussed. To him the game was simply a tax loss but it turned into great a gift idea during the holiday season, particularly as an educational toy for pre-teens. The previous year the game had actually shown a profit.

"That's partly because it's been recalled. After your divorce, they replaced the old 'wife' piece with the new 'actress/model' piece and took away half of the money and the best hotels," said the Banker.

"I'd rather play monopoly," said the Junior Vice President.

"So would Will Bates," answered the Banker.

"To paraphrase our situation, you don't really have any tangible assets that we really want," stated the Senior Vice President.

"However, we will take the Airline and several of your rental properties. Since it is against New York state law for a bank to be associated with gaming institutions, we've created a small holding company to operate them temporarily. The other more junior creditors will be allowed to litigate for them and the remaining rental properties," stated the Junior Vice President.

"Those are all of my assets. I guess I can go," said Donald, glibly.

"Those are not your greatest assets. *You* are your greatest asset," said the Banker.

Donald smiled at the compliment. The Banker continued, "We want you to work for us to help pay off your debt."

"You mean manage my properties?" asked Donald.

"Possibly," said the Banker.

"Maybe improving your real estate and mortgage portfolio," said Donald, licking his lips. He had a gleam in his eyes, a predatory gleam like a lion among limping zebras.

Now, the nearly ten billion dollars of mortgages and business loans would be at his feet to plunder as he so desired. Bankruptcy can be fun, especially if your creditors are really stupid and believe that you're honest.

"A personal service contract to me," stated the Banker.

"I'll sign it after I read it," said Donald.

"Read away," said the Junior Vice President, handing Donald the contract.

Donald hastily read the contract and signed it. He smiled and joked with the vice presidents. However, the Banker stood aside reading the contract and smiling secretively. *Donald Clubs may be Master of the Deal but he is certainly not master of the fine print.*

The other bankers left and a photographer arrived and set up his camera. The Banker asked Donald to strip to his shorts. Donald asked, "Am I posing for 'Cosmopolitan' or 'Men's Good Health' magazine? I guess they want brains as well as good beef cake."

The Banker only smiled. Then the photographer took Donald's picture while the broke billionaire adopted what he thought was a sexy pose. Donald continued to pose flexing his not too fit middle-aged muscles but acting like he's a sexy twenty-year old. The photographer kept clicking the shutter with an almost idiotic smile on his face. The Banker tossed Donald a pair of handcuffs and said, "Try these on, they'll make you even sexier."

Donald laughed. "An S and M magazine. Cool! Guess which one I am."

"An S," replied the Banker.

The photographer suggested, "Let's take a few shots in the elevator. The cramped, sterile space will enhance the intimacy and the eroticism of the pictures. We could go to the parking garage and take some pictures in your car. It's a Bentley, right? That would very sexy."

Clubs nodded and adopted a pose that should be reserved for the Terminator alone. No one else has quite the body. But Donald thought he had.

"Maybe for autoerotics," replied the Banker.

They led him to the elevator, which whisked him down to the parking garage level at the basement of building.

Before the elevator doors opened at the parking garage level, the Banker entered a four-digit code into the elevator's keypad and the elevator continued to descend.

The elevator doors opened on a brown utility door labeled 'Auxiliary Power.' The Banker explained that this room provided electric power for the building.

Donald asked, "You mean I'm going to supervise the staff down here?"

The Banker nodded. "You're going to work here."

The Banker opened the door and entered the rear of a room that looked like the lower deck of an ancient Roman galley. There were over a dozen wooden benches with associated oars, manned by well over two-dozen slaves, each dressed in basketball shorts and sweaty T-shirts. The slaves were of all ages, sexes and races. Each was shackled to their bench.

At the front of the room was digital watt meter. Since it only had a two-digit capacity, the maximum reading was 99KW. It was presently reading 14KW.

In front of the meter stood a skinny red-haired woman dressed as a dominatrix and wearing a mask like the Lone Ranger. She was beating a huge kettledrum very slowly but also very resolutely, "BOOM, boom." She seemed to be enjoying herself immensely.

Grunting, sweating and straining, the slaves pulled their oars in unison with the drums. They did this very well simply because they had had a lot of practice.

The Banker and his little entourage started to stroll slowly to the front of the erstwhile galley. Then he went around to one of the slaves and asked, "What's your first name and why are you here?"

"Roger and I embezzled $50,000," said a thin but wiry male slave.

"Are there any other embezzlers here?" asked the Banker.

The skinny woman struck the drum again. "BOOM, boom." The slaves moved the oars perfectly, almost as if they were a single person.

Several hands went up and the banker asked, "How much?"

"$100,000," replied a skinny black male slave.

"$25,000," a thin white female slave called out.

"BOOM, boom." Again, the oars moved in perfect rhythm.

The banker pointed at another female slave and she answered, "I didn't pay my dues for the coffee club and I ate all the donuts, anyway."

She was both somewhat voluptuous and moderately attractive. Her sad brown eyes met those of the Banker and seemed to plead for redemption.

"That stuff's fattening, no wonder you're here," replied the Banker.

"BOOM, boom." The oars again moved in unison.

"And you?" asked banker.

"I took kickbacks from construction contractors," replied a muscular male slave.

"What did you do wrong?" asked the Banker.

"I claimed on my resume that I had an MBA and I didn't," said one of the slaves.

The banker pointed to another slave in the same row who responded, "I said that I went to Harvard on my resume and I didn't go to Harvard. I went to Memphis State."

"BOOM, boom." The oars again moved in perfect order.

"And you?" asked the Banker.

"I stole soap from the janitors," said a young, very nerdy-looking man. "I was going to return it," he continued, almost sobbing.

"BOOM, boom." The oars again moved in almost perfect order. The oar of the nerd was slightly late.

The Banker shook his finger at the nerd. "Naughty, naughty."

"What about you?" asked the Banker.

"I told people my online degree was from a real university," said a young, slightly chubby female slave.

"Was it from Clubs Online University?" asked the Banker.

"Yes," she answered.

"We want real degrees from real schools, not Junior Colleges, not online, no life experience credit allowed. When you work for me you're going to earn your money and that starts with your education," ranted the Banker.

"BOOM, boom." The oars again moved perfectly.

The Banker pointed out a group of about a dozen middle-aged male slaves at the front of the room. These slaves had an extra set of shackles on them and oversized oars. They seemed to be straining much harder to pull their oars than the others. The Banker looked at them and said, "These are businessmen who defaulted on their loans to us and tried to obtain protection under chapter 11 of the bankruptcy code."

"BOOM, boom." Again, the oars moved perfectly.

"Who are the people with the duct tape over their mouths?" asked Donald.

"Those were their silent partners."

"BOOM, boom." This time one of the oars was very late. The embezzler pulling the oar looked at the Banker and said with a sheepish grin, "Never mind."

A large, muscular, bare-chested man in running shoes, black sweat pants and wearing a mask cracked his bullwhip over the head of the embezzler. He said, "First time's a warning. Next time's for real."

"BOOM, boom." The oars moved perfectly again. The slaves were resynchronized.

"Who's he, the guy with the whip?" asked Donald.

"He's the head of Human Resources," replied the Banker.

"BOOM, boom." The oars swept with almost perfect timing. The embezzler led the sweep very slightly.

"Who's the woman on the drums?" asked Donald Clubs.

"A Temp. A Kelly girl, I think," said the Banker.

As they walked along the rows of benches, the banker asked the remaining slaves about their offenses. Several recounted their crimes to the banker and his small entourage. Their offenses ranged from kickbacks on construction contracts to nepotism to improper use of the Xerox machine.

Donald Clubs was duly impressed by the ruthlessness of the Banker and said, "When I get back on top, I want you to work for me. You can discipline my staff and work force. You might help me get my net worth over that of Will Bates and I'll be the richest man in the world."

"BOOM, boom." The oars swept with almost perfect timing. The soap thief led the sweep. The Banker may have scared him enough to generate some adrenalin.

The Banker thought, *that certainly makes this a lot easier.* He then said, "It's not a matter of '**when**,' it's more a question of '**if**.'"

"What does that mean? I'm going to supervise these slugs, aren't I?" asked Donald.

"You **are** one of the slugs, the biggest one in fact," said the Banker.

"You can't do this to me. I'm management, an entrepreneur," said Donald Clubs.

"You signed a contract, a personal service contract to me. Since I can't or won't find you a management job, you'll have to take the job that I give you," said the Banker.

"BOOM, boom." The oars swept perfectly.

"I'll call my lawyer. He'll break the contract," said the near naked real estate speculator.

"First, how are you going to pay him? You're broke, bankrupt. You don't have any money. If you do, I get it before any lawyer does and you go to jail for fraud. And no one is going to help you pro bono, not after all the scummy, ruthless things you've done," replied the Banker.

"Like what?" asked Donald.

"Like when you kicked out those poor minority tenants from those apartment buildings on the East Side so you could remake their homes into upscale yuppie condos," said the Banker.

"That was just business," answered Donald.

"So's this," answered the Banker.

"BOOM, boom." The oars swept perfectly.

"Secondly, how are you going to contact him? Do you see any pay phones? Cell phones? Computers?" continued the Banker.

"Thirdly, who would believe you? Especially with your reputation for extreme, almost annoying, flamboyancy and your flaunting of recreational drugs. You're here for the duration. Besides, over the long run, it may save you money on liposuction. You'll get rid of that fat the old-fashioned way," said the Banker.

"BOOM, boom." The oars swept imperfectly. It seemed that the other rowers were listening in.

"No, you can't!" Donald entreated.

The banker, photographer and the HR whip man dragged Donald, dumbfounded but still struggling, to the front bench. The skinny drum-beater yelled, "Coffee break!"

She rushed to help with the struggling Donald. The rowers collapsed and the meter dropped to 0. She gave the photographer the keys to Donald's shackles and helped him lock Donald in.

While Donald sat in his new home, alternately sobbing, cursing, threatening and trying to break his chains, the HR whip man and the drummer girl passed out steaming mugs of liquid to the slaves. All the slaves complained about the taste, but they all emptied their mugs.

After the mugs were emptied, the drummer woman and the HR whip man collected them. The rowers rested a few minutes and then a yellow light below the digit meter lit up and the HR whip man rushed to the back of the galley and yelled, "Coffee break's over, back on your heads."

The drummer woman screamed, "Idle speed." Despite her short stature and scrawny build there was power, force and determination in her high pitched but still imposing voice. She started beating the drum slowly and deliberately, "Boom, boom." The rowers responded raggedly. Everyone was out of sync for the first three to five beats, which came at five-second intervals. The digital watt meter slowly equilibrated at 7KW.

She looked at a computer screen in front of her and said to the HR whip man, "They're using the Xerox machine on the fourth floor."

The HR whip man said, "We need more power." and cracked his whip.

The drummer woman screamed, "Cruising speed." She beat the drum more quickly, more deliberately and loudly. "Boom, boom." The rowers picked up the pace and got synchronized after only one or two beats. The beats came at two-second intervals and the digital watt meter reading rapidly reached 15KW.

Clubs sat there dumbfounded until the HR whip man told him, "I will enforce one rule; if you don't row, you don't eat or get anywhere near enough water. It's very unpleasant down here without enough water."

The drummer woman added, "Without water you might just not make it out of here."

Donald started to row, incompetently, slowly and out of step. But both the drummer woman and the HR whip man let it slip temporarily except for snickering at the great entrepreneur and threatening to tell the Banker. Donald was obviously out of shape, poorly coordinated, out of practice and straining to keep up with the more experienced rowers.

The drummer woman looked at her computer screen and said, "They're turning up the air conditioner on the seventh floor."

"We need more power," replied the HR whip man.

The drummer woman screamed, "**Flank speed.**" The power in her voice would intimidate anyone even Donald Clubs, even when he owned a large fraction of Manhattan and Northern New Jersey. She beat the drum more quickly and very loudly, "**BOOM**, BOOM." The other rowers again picked up the pace and synchronized after only one beat. Donald strained at his oars and eventually got synchronized with the rest of the rowers. The beats now came at approximately one-second intervals. The digital watt meter moved to 27 within seconds and then went to 29 when Donald finally got with the program.

The drummer woman looked at her computer screen again and screamed with raw emotion in her voice, "**Battle speed**." Her voice sent fear down the spine of Donald Clubs and he tried desperately to comply with her wishes. She now beat the drum at a frenzied pace and at an overwhelming volume. "**BOOM, BOOM**." The rowers strained to pick up the pace. The beats came at less than one- second intervals. Within seconds the digital watt meter moved up to 42.

Donald was really exhausted but did his best to keep up. He had a good reason to do so. He could hear the HR whip man cracking his bullwhip behind him and the screams of its victims echoed in his ears. He even saw small amounts of slave blood flying through the air. Fear-generated-adrenalin fueled him.

The drummer woman again screamed, "**Ram speed**." She was now beating the drum at nearly demonic pace and at deafening volume. "**BOOM, BOOM**." She was pounding on the drum so hard and fast that she dripped with sweat.

The rowers somehow picked up the pace and got synchronized after only a few beats despite the fact it was obvious that they had been pushed nearly to their limits. The beats were coming at approximately half-second intervals. The digital watt meter moved to 55 but it took over ten seconds to do so.

A terrified Donald rowed with all his might. He wasn't doing a great job but at least he didn't get whipped. The HR whip man explained why. "The boss won't let me beat you the first day, but I'll credit your account, if you know what I mean."

Between beats the drummer woman made unfriendly, obscene gestures at him. He was certainly not among friends.

After a near eternity at Ram speed, the drummer woman yelled "**Cruising Speed**." She slowed the beat rate to one every two seconds. The digital watt meter decreased to 24 after the rowers resynchronized.

Then she yelled, "**Idle Speed**." and lowered the beat rate to one every five seconds. The rowers resynchronized at the lower speed and Donald started to breathe easier.

The drummer woman yelled, "Dinner time." Donald looked around and saw that everyone was soaked in sweat, the rowers, the drummer woman and the HR whip man from whipping slow or incompetent oarsmen. The evidence for the whipping was readily apparent. There was blood splattered on the benches in several locations and on a least a handful of the rowers.

Finally, the HR man with the whip said, "All clear, time to eat."

Donald looked exhausted and very much in pain. He certainly wasn't used to this kind of hard exercise.

The drummer woman/dominatrix stopped beating the drum and started passing around little cardboard buckets of food. Each bucket had its own distinctive and noxious odor. A female embezzler said, "I got gruel, does anyone have any swill?"

Another answered, "I got swill. I prefer slop."

"I got slop. But I'd rather have gruel," replied a bankrupt businessman.

The female embezzler looked at the bankrupt businessman and said, "I'll give you my gruel for your slop, and then trade the slop for his swill." She pointed to her fellow embezzler. "OK?"

"No Trading! What do you think this is Club Med? A luxury ocean liner?" shouted the HR whip man.

"You mean like the Titanic?" asked another bankrupt businessman.

"Yes, like the Titanic!" said the HR whip man.

"C'mon Iceberg," said the woman with the online degree.

"Gimme an 'I,'" said the lady without her MBA.

Everybody said, "I." Even the silent partners mumbled.

"Gimme a 'C'" said the lady without her MBA.

"Quiet, or you won't get your dirt for desert," said the HR whip man.

"Don't take away our dirt, it's even better than boogers," said the donut thief.

They stuck an IV in the arm of one of the silent partners. Then the drummer girl removed the tape from over his mouth and he said, "Yummy, glucose."

"What do I get to eat?" asked Donald.

"You'll be last, so you'll probably get road kill or a leftover skunk sandwich," said the skinny dominatrix.

"Oh God! This place is worse than hell," said Donald in despair. He used to think of himself as gourmet in his previous life.

"I like it," said the HR whip man.

"So do I," said the drummer woman.

"I hope they put me down here permanently," continued the drummer woman.

"How can I get out of here? Tell me, please," begged Donald.

Then the door opened and two men and a little girl carrying a small jingling coffee can walked in. The little girl looked at the donut thief and yelled ecstatically, "Mommy!"

One of the men counted out the change and small bills in the coffee can. He said, "$28.40."

The Banker looked at a clipboard on the small table in front of the kettledrums and said, "OK, let her go."

The drummer woman unlocked the shackles of the donut thief who rushed, sobbing with joy, to the outstretched arms of her daughter who said, "I collected from my paper route early. I love you, Mommy. Can I have a pony now?"

The HR whip man gave her a plastic bag containing her clothes and belongings. The cadre of the galley wished her good luck and *bon appétit*.

The banker was handed a cashier's check from Physical Bank for $58,457,000, which he showed to Donald. He then compared it to the clipboard and smiling he said, "That's how you get out of here. You buy your way out. This amount of money will buy freedom for this bankrupt businessman and his silent partner."

Just behind Clubs, the drummer woman and the HR whip man unlocked the shackles for a silent partner and a businessman in the row behind him. They were handed large plastic bags holding their business suits, watches and wallets. The bankrupt businessman asked, "We owed you only $54,200,000, why did you require over 58 million?"

"Interest, we bankers are obsessed by interest. It's our stock-in-trade," said the Banker.

"There's one bad thing about being able to buy your way out, you must do it quickly. As the other rowers buy their way out and leave, the interface between the oars and the generator must be modified to maintain the required power level. Simply put, the more people leave, the harder you have to pull the oars," said the Banker.

There was a look of near terror in Donald Clubs' eyes as he looked at the banker. "Let's make a deal." He then gulped, without water, a pill hidden in a small pocket in his shorts.

The Banker thought, 'Making a deal with Donald Clubs is the equivalent of playing with hungry lions while wearing a pork chop suit.' He said, "No deal, just pay us what you owe with interest."

The Banker left the basement after whispering some advice to the drummer woman, who nodded her approval.

Only a few minutes before the end of dinner, Donald heard behind him one of the women slaves say, "Yummy, dirt!"

"This is the best dirt I've ever had! It's even got some delicious worms in it," said another.

Donald almost retched; he had been eating road kill and would be lucky to get dirt or nothing at all. Donald relented. He must have realized that he would not able to spend his money, star on his two television shows, escort his actress/models or run his online university in his underwear while rowing a fake Roman warship in this little approximation of hell. He called to the HR whip man who then contacted the Banker. When the Banker arrived, the galley was already up to 'Cruising Speed' and Donald was rapidly becoming exhausted again. Donald said to the

Banker, "Get my laptop in my penthouse. It has a list of all my offshore and Suisse accounts including amounts and passwords. The logon id is 'Alexander' and the password is 'TheGreatest.' Please let me out of here."

"Not 'till the checks clear," said the Banker.

"Please, Please, Please, Pretty Please," begged Donald.

"Remember those people who sued you for building on their property and not paying for it? You let your lawyers get continuance after continuance so you didn't have to litigate because you'd probably lose? You'll have to wait just like them," said the Banker.

The Banker turned and walked up to the drummer woman and whispered something in her ear. She screamed, **"Ram Speed."**

Two hours later, the banker returned with two other men, one was carrying an oxygen bottle, the other the big plastic bag with Donald's suit in it. Donald was exhausted, at the end of his rope and had a wild, desperate look in his eyes.

He asked, "Did the money transfer arrive? Can I get out of here? Please, Please, Please."

"It did, but you have to do one more thing before you can go," replied the Banker.

"What's that?" asked Donald.

"Clap your hands twice and say, 'Fannie Mae, Fannie Mae, there's no place like the home, there's no place like the home," said the Banker.

"That's really stupid!" said Donald.

"Yes, but it is a prerequisite. Do you want to get out of here or not?" asked the HR whip man.

Immediately, Donald clapped his hands twice and said, "Fannie Mae, Fannie Mae, there's no place like the home, there's no place like the home."

They unfastened his shackles and gave him his clothes. He dressed quickly then took a big breath out of the oxygen bottle.

A few hours later at the banker's hotel room, the Banker greeted a very tall, extremely attractive female executive at the door of his hotel room. The executive hoped that somehow, she could wrangle a date with him and maybe seduce him. To her, power was an aphrodisiac and besides that the Banker was taller, better looking and better built than Clubs and disarmingly funny as well. After all, she was as tall as a model and almost as attractive. Then she noticed he was wearing a simple but tasteful and elegant platinum wedding band. *No matter,* she thought, *he probably collects actress/models on the side. A vice president might make an interesting trophy.*

Then the drummer woman knocked on the door and entered carrying several cardboard buckets. She removed the cheap raincoat covering her leather outfit and made her report. "Clubs overdosed on his designer drug less than a block from the bank. You shouldn't take those drugs on an empty stomach or when you're dehydrated, or exhausted, out of shape or all of the above."

"Is he all right?" asked the Banker.

"He'll be OK but he'll spend the next two weeks in the Mount Sinai substance abusers ward," said the drummer woman.

"He keeps saying, 'Soylent Green is people,'" continued the Drummer Woman.

"I'm glad he's getting treatment, particularly in a good hospital. We'll pay for that. This does have a bonus for us, now no one will ever believe anything he says about being a galley slave. I'm going to send him a fruit basket before he gets out," said the Banker.

"Donald is very amoral but not totally evil," said the Drummer Woman.

"He's a lot less bad than some of the people we've dealt with," said the Banker.

"Some of those guys would've used him as an end table," said the drummer woman.

The attractive executive noticed that drummer woman was wearing a matching platinum wedding ring. The drummer woman was short, about 5'1", and a skinny eighty pounds soaking wet. She also had a plain rodent-like but not unpleasant face, a skinny hour-glass figure ruined by very small breasts. Her legs were thin but shapely. Unfortunately, they were slightly asymmetric due to her small but very noticeable limp.

The beautiful VP wondered why such a rich desirable man would marry a homely, crippled, little woman like her instead of escorting actress/models or even herself?

"How did the funds transfer turn out?" asked the Banker.

"I've paid off all of Donald's debts. The two pension funds have been restored. I've set up a fund to reimburse the seven small businesses that Donald refused to pay. The bank's loan has been repaid with interest."

"That's good' there'll be seven less bankruptcies and no layoffs at the bank. I think we've done our job," said the Banker.

65

"There's money left over too—seventy-eight million. What do we do with it?" asked the Accountant.

"First, we pay the caterer," said the Drummer Woman.

The beautiful female executive gasped, "What?"

"You don't think that the Manhattan Rowing Society and all those off-Broadway actors would help us without being fed, do you?" asked the Drummer Woman.

"It was relatively cheap, $475.00 at about $15.00 per serving. The gruel was Manhattan Clam Chowder. The swill was New England Clam Chowder. Slop was Shrimp Stew - all from Mike's Seafood Palace. You know the one with 3 stars. I brought some back, we can microwave them and have dinner in. Then we can start playtime a little earlier," said the Drummer Woman with a kittenish gleam in her eyes.

The creamy patina on the platinum wedding bands said that the honeymoon had been long over, but the look in their eyes said that it certainly wasn't. The executive also noticed that the pathetic skinny woman smelled of sweat rather than perfume yet it gave her an earthy sensuality.

"What about Road kill?" asked the Banker.

"That was Kentucky Fried Chicken—original recipe. There was no Skunk sandwich, although if I had to, I'd make him one with peanut butter," answered the Drummer Woman.

"What's dirt?" asked the beautiful VP.

"I made that. It's chocolate desert topping mixed with crushed Oreo cookies, chocolate sprinkles and gummy worms. A great desert," stated the skinny Drummer Woman. "I learned how to make it at that garden club you made me join," she continued.

"That $78 million is yours, a finder's fee," said the beautiful executive.

"I really don't need it. Use some of it to pay off Donald's penthouse. Nobody should lose their home not even Donald. I'll set up a small, say $5,000, checking account for him, with my own money."

"**Our** money, remember," interjected the skinny woman, "You've been a naughty boy, I'm on top tonight."

"Use the rest to pay off his debts from his previous bankruptcies. I've had the bank's HR department write a memorandum so he can collect unemployment insurance. He gets to start over, but the middle-class way. If necessary, I'll try to get him a job at our university. They always need help in the business department. Teaching physics is my real profession," said the Banker, looking at the beautiful executive and beaming at skinny Drummer Woman.

"You don't want 78 million?" asked the Accountant.

"Nope," said the Banker.

"If he bankrupted you, he'd show you no mercy," stated the Accountant.

"I'm not him," said Banker/Physicist.

"Thank God," said the Drummer Woman, eating her dirt.

THE END

About the Author

Dennis Charles

Dennis Charles is retired nuclear scientist with 3 master's degrees. He worked in commercial nuclear power for over 20 years where he acquired a detailed knowledge of nuclear reactors and Corporate America as well. He also worked in the Department of Energy's Nuclear Nonproliferation group for 4 years where he obtained a good working knowledge of nuclear weapons design, deployment and manufacture. He also worked in the Aerospace industry for 2 years and a year in information technology. He spent 5 years teaching freshman physics and general science at a number of college and Universities.

He considers himself a total failure and loser because he doesn't have a Ferrari and a 90-pound trophy wife. All has to show for his life is one lousy Nobel Prize. Since the Nobel Prize money must be spent on humanitarian causes he can't even spend it unless he can get his favorite Fort Myers strip joints and the Naples Mercedes dealership declared 3rd world countries.

His present hobbies are watching DVDs and Judge Judy, doing Astrophysics and writing. He has written a collection of short stories titled The Weiner Dogs of War available on Amazon. It's about little talking dogs: mostly dachshunds, toy poodles and other tiny lapdogs that fight King Kong, king Cobras, dinosaurs, saber-toothed tigers, vampires and monsters from outer space.

If you think that talking dachshunds make strange heroes, you should read the next stories from the soon to be released collections on Amazon: The Civil Nuclear War, Several Days in May and Flying the Unfriendly Skies.

BEING OF SOUND MIND AND BODY....

A Short Story

Vincent D'Angelo

The old man sat at the aged wood desk in the den. He leaned back in the well-worn swivel chair with his hands behind his head—comforted in having finished writing checks for the month's bills. Gazing through the window, he saw a half-moon shining brightly in the middle of a starry sky. The serenity helped him collect his thoughts.

He was reasonably content as a retired senior citizen but things never were the same since Ma passed. How could they be? They had rarely ever spent a day apart since the day they were married. But it is what it is, he thought, and there's little I can do about it.

He missed Ma something dreadful, but kept it to himself. He didn't want to be a source of sadness to his two children, Danny and Sheila and the grandkids, Sheila's seven-year-old Mark and Danny's nine-year-old Stacey. He loved hearing the grandkids call him Grampa. Even Danny and Sheila referred to him in the same way. The only problem was he didn't hear it often enough.

Household chores and repairs around the house kept him busy, his mind occupied. The house was old, but he was handy with tools and able to keep it in reasonably good shape. Dinner dishes were his last chore of the day. After they were done, he would spend the rest of the evening relaxing in his favorite stuffed chair in front of the television, his energy having been spent on the efforts of the day. Considering everything, life was good.

If he had anything to complain about, it was the loneliness. Danny and Sheila and their children lived several hours away in the big city, too far away for visits other than Christmas, Thanksgiving, and his birthday. The only other contact he had with them was the occasional phone call. They would usually have the grandkids make the calls and from the background, they would call out to say hello and that they would call him soon themselves. But they rarely did.

When Danny or Sheila did call they were always in the midst of something or about to rush off somewhere and couldn't stay on the phone long. He understood. They were wrapped up in their busy family lives and careers and too preoccupied.

On those special occasions when they were all together, Danny and Sheila would tell him he needed to get out and socialize. They reminded him there were a lot of opportunities for older people to socialize: the Senior Citizen's Club, church socials, senior outings and more. But, he never could get used to doing things without Ma at his side. So he kept to himself.

He knew Danny and Sheila cared about him because they were always after him to get regular check-ups, make sure to take his vitamins, and to eat healthy. He'd always agreed, but rarely followed their advice. He was over eighty years old and felt well enough. As far as he was concerned, that's what really mattered. What better indication of a person's health could there be?

Lately, their calls had become even less frequent. He had decided that he would no longer call them. They would have to call him. But he realized by doing so he would only be punishing himself.

Then he had a brainwave, an idea that he believed was so clever he became all excited. It was a little mischievous he admitted, but he felt it was justified. On one of their visits, he overheard his daughter mention the word, inheritance. It made him feel kind of sad but he shrugged it off. It was, after all, a fact of life. The older generations had the money and the newer generations needed money.

His idea was a simple one but he was sure it would get them calling. He would write his 'last will and testament' and state that whoever made the last call to him before he died would inherit his house and money. These days, even little kids are motivated by money—always sticking their hands out asking their parents for it. He chuckled mischievously at the thought that, although it wasn't much, one of the children might get the entire inheritance.

The new-fangled phone they had given him last Christmas—something he hadn't really needed—kept a record of the last incoming call. There would be no question about which one of them made the final call. He laughed to himself already imagining his phone ringing off the hook. *It could be little Mark that would end up with the inheritance money. How funny is that?* he thought. He didn't care that there was a bit of sadistic humor in the plan, as long as the phone calls came.

He spun his chair around to the desk and began to peck out the audacious will on the trusty old Underwood. He made carbon copies, one for each of his children, one for his lawyer, and one for the metal box in the bottom draw of the desk where he kept his important papers.

He knew how Last Wills began; he had seen it many times in the movies and on television: "Being of sound mind and body . . ."

He knew that when they read it, Danny and Sheila would think he had surely become senile. He knew they already suspected that. He was certain his lawyer would call him and try to persuade him make a more conventional will, but nothing was going change his mind. It was *his* idea and he was certain it would accomplish what he wanted.

Tomorrow morning, he would stop over to the widow Krautsmeyer who lived next door and have her sign it as a witness to make it legal and binding. He didn't know much about legal matters but he recalled from the television and movies this was the way it was supposed to be done. After

71

she signed it, he would go to the post office and mail a copy to each of his children and a copy to his lawyer.

He felt good knowing he had accomplished two things: He had made a will—something he had put off doing—and best of all, it created a reason for the kids and grandkids to call him.

The following day, the widow Krautsmeyer signed the will for him. He was so elated with his idea and so energized by it, he decided to walk to the post office rather than drive; besides, the walk would do him good. He knew that he was not walking as much as he should. He would make up for the many walks he had missed by walking faster than usual, double-time as they had him do when he was in the army. And off he went.

The widow Krautsmeyer watched him through the curtains as he left. She saw he was walking very fast and could hear him calling out, "Hup-two-three-four. Hup-two-three…."

Half hour later, she saw him coming back. He was not walking fast now; actually, walking quite slowly. She watched him for a bit and just as she was about to turn away from the window, she saw him suddenly stop. He put his hands to his chest and opened his mouth wide like he was gasping for air. He took a few staggering steps forward, then fell to the pavement. She ran towards the door to help him, then stopped and ran to first call 9-1-1. She ran back to the door, stopped again and ran to the kitchen to fill a glass with water.

The widow Krautsmeyer was a former nurse. As soon as she reached him, she put a finger to his neck. No pulse. The old man was gone. *He must have had a heart attack,* she thought. There was nothing she could do for him. The EMS people arrived quickly. After making an attempt to revive him, right there on the sidewalk, where he'd fallen, they covered him with a blanket, placed him on a gurney and raised his lifeless body into the ambulance.

When the lawyer received his copy of the will, he had already heard of his client's passing. He had the sheriff come with him to the house, where they collected the phone and took it back to the sheriff's office.

A few days after the funeral, the lawyer called the children for a meeting at his office for the reading of their father's will. The grieving Danny and Sheila came for the will reading; their spouses remained home to watch the children.

When they were seated, Sheila and Danny whispered to each other wondering why the sheriff was standing in the lawyer's office.

The attorney opened the discussion with a brief talk on the laws of the state pertaining to wills. After he finished, he told them that he and the sheriff had activated the call memory on their father's phone in the presence of other witnesses and had ascertained who had made the last call. Danny and Sheila looked puzzled and asked the lawyer what the phone had to do with anything.

"Are you not aware of the will?" the attorney asked.

"Dad had a will?" they both asked in surprise.

"Didn't you read the copy of the will he sent you?" He pointed out that it said at the bottom of the will they each would receive copies.

Again, they both spoke at the same time saying that after they learned their father had died, they were too despondent to bother reading any of their mail.

Their response was followed by a long silence, during which the lawyer kept looking around the room as though trying to formulate his thoughts. He looked down at his desk and began to read the brief will. He recited what their father had written and then summarized it. "It says whoever made the last call to him will inherit his entire estate."

"I don't understand," Danny muttered.

"What does it all mean?" Sheila asked.

"Simply put, it means, you and your families will not be receiving any inheritance," the lawyer said somberly.

Danny and Sheila looked at each other in shock. They started talking at the same time, saying the same thing: their father wasn't rich but he had money and assets. They knew a lot about his finances, his savings, the house, everything. How could they not receive any of it, they asked?

"Your father's will states that everything, meaning his savings, his life insurance, the house, everything, would go to just one person, the person who had made the last phone call to him." The attorney hesitated. "The sheriff went with me to your father's house as a witness to check the phone to determine who made the last call . . ." He hesitated once again. "It was not a family member."

Danny and Sheila looked at each other, confused and in disbelief.

"What *does* this all mean?" asked Danny.

"Your father neglected to state in the will that it only applied to family members. Someone else, a stranger, made the last call. That person is legally entitled to everything your father left."

When their initial shock subsided, Danny said they would contest it. The lawyer explained that it was irrefutable and uncontestable. He told them in no uncertain terms that it would be costly to challenge and there was no chance they would prevail. "The person who made the last call is entitled to the entire estate," the lawyer insisted.

They sat dumbstruck, disbelieving, but the attorney's adamancy made them realize it was true.

After they had calmed down, Sheila and Danny asked who had made the last call. Hearing that, the sheriff left the office and went to the waiting room. The lawyer explained the sheriff had contacted the person and she was in the waiting room.

Danny leaned over to Sheila and whispered not to worry, he was sure that whoever it was would give the money to them because it was rightfully theirs. It was obvious it was what their father had intended. After all, it was just a simple mistake made by a senile, elderly man.

The sheriff held the door open to let in a slim, petite young lady with stringy, blond hair, wearing a floral, ankle length, bargain store cotton dress that looked like it had been laundered a few too many times. She was holding a small child in her arms and a little boy was holding on to her skirt.

She looked frightened as if she were being brought before a courtroom judge. The sheriff brought over a chair for her. She sat on the edge of it.

The lawyer introduced the young lady as Jane Miller. She smiled nervously and nodded politely to each of them as they were introduced. In a quiet voice she introduced the baby, Melissa, and the boy, Josh, as though not wanting them to be overlooked.

The attorney then said that Jane Miller was the one who had made that last call. Before anyone could ask the obvious question about why she had called their father, the attorney waved his hand in her direction.

She hesitated a moment and looked down at the toddler who was still holding on to her skirt and then at the child with a thumb in its mouth. She spoke in a small, anxious voice.

"I had meant to call Social Services. I needed to know something about my food stamps. But I accidentally dialed a wrong number." She said nothing further.

The attorney gestured for her to continue. He said, kindly, "Please speak up so we can hear you clearly."

"When I realized I had dialed a wrong number, I apologized to the man that answered and was going to hang up. But the friendly man on the phone said there was no need to apologize, at his age, he often dialed wrong numbers." She hesitated, looking reflective. "He said he was hoping the call might be from one of his children or his grandchildren. But he was happy to have someone, anyone, to talk with.

"I told him that I was happy to speak with him and that it was a pleasant change from *my* always being the needy one. We both laughed. He asked if I had any children. I said yes, six months old Melissa and three years old Josh. The nice man said, 'That's wonderful,' that he loved children and had children and grandchildren whom he loved dearly but didn't get to talk to or see them often enough. We bid each other good day." She paused. "It was a short, pleasant conversation. After we hung up, I felt sad for him."

The lawyer asked Melissa to take the children out of the room so that he and his clients could talk privately. After everyone had filed out of the room, the attorney asked Danny and Sheila for their thoughts.

"I don't feel hostile towards the girl," Sheila said, "but I would expect that she would give up any claim on our father's estate. After all, it was just a mistake!"

"I'm sorry," the lawyer said, "but she hasn't given any indication she's going to do that. She would have offered it by now."

"Is there any chance she might change her mind?" Danny asked.

"I doubt it," the attorney replied.

Danny and Sheila both said they'd agree to give her a token sum if she did. If she did not accept their offer, they would like to contest the will.

"I assure you, that by law, it's unquestionable; the inheritance belongs to the young lady. If you're thinking of getting a second opinion, you're welcome to do so, but as an attorney, I'm certain this is an open and shut case."

Sheila asked, "Why would anyone who knows they're the accidental beneficiary of a windfall, in good conscience, keep the money?"

With a solemn face the attorney offered, "I happen to know something about her circumstances. Perhaps, someone who's been dealt a bad hand all their life isn't disposed to pass up an opportunity. Perhaps thinking of it as . . . well, divine intervention." He hesitated. "Without the money, it's obvious your lives wouldn't be affected measurably. However, for Mrs. Miller, it's a different story. The poor girl is a destitute widow. If it'll make you feel better, since she is the recipient of the money, I'll suggest she pay all the legal fees. I'm sure she will agree."

They left the lawyer's office. His parting remark was if anything should change, he would let them know. His words had a hollow ring.

The next day, the attorney's young assistant came by each of their homes with some papers for them to sign. "If we don't sign, would this be our ace-in-the-hole?" Danny asked. The assistant said if they didn't sign, it could lead to a futile lawsuit and they'd be obligated for the legal costs for both sides.

Sheila and Danny finally accepted that it was over, signed the document and moved on from the inheritance that wasn't to be.

A few weeks later, they each received a call from the widow Krautsmeyer. She told them there was considerable work being done on the house, both inside and out. She saw a slim, young blond lady in discussions with the workman. From the widow's description, it was Jane Miller. Neither Sheila nor Danny expressed interest and told her they never wanted to see the old house again.

They didn't live near it so it would be out-of-sight and out-of-mind for them and would exist only in the fond memories of their childhood.

Several months later, each of them received a letter from Jane Miller. It was a hand-written invitation for them to come and spend the following Sunday with her and her children at the house and she asked that they bring their children. The letter included her phone number. They weren't going to accept the invitation. However, curiosity got the better of them.

Sheila and Danny walked up the familiar pathway that led up to the house, accompanied by their children and their spouses.

They were brought up in this house. Now, freshly painted and newly landscaped, it no longer looked like the old weathered house that it had become through the years. It looked like the home they remembered from their childhood.

Jane Miller came down the walkway to greet them. Walking in front of her was her son Josh. She was holding baby Melissa's hand as the toddler stumbled along attempting to walk. They were all dressed in what appeared to be their Sunday finest, although the mother certainly didn't seem to have spent much of the money on herself. She was still wearing a bargain store dress; just a new version of the one she had worn in the lawyer's office. Her lack of self-indulgence didn't go by them unnoticed.

It was only one of the many surprises that would come that day.

Inside the home, they received more of a shock than a surprise when they saw, hanging above the fireplace mantel, an oil painting of their father. They recognized it to be the one their mother had had painted from a photo of him. Grampa stored it in the basement, saying he had no intention of hanging it in their home and had offered it to Danny and Sheila. But neither one had gotten around to picking it up. They both pretty much forgot about it.

"I know it wasn't right for me to keep it, but I hung your father's picture there to put a face to the voice I remembered so well," Jane Miller said in an almost apologetic tone. "You can take the painting with you when you leave."

Danny's wife Martha, the more outspoken member of the family, asked Jane Miller about the children's own grandparents. Jane explained that she had spent her entire childhood in an orphanage and never knew her parents. Jane's pleasant look turned sorrowful. "My husband John was killed in an automobile accident. He was a machinist in a factory and had been working double shifts to earn extra money. He fell asleep at the wheel on the way home and hit a tree. We had no insurance." She paused. "We met when we were both children living in the orphanage so there weren't any relatives for me to turn to."

She explained that after the accident, she worked cleaning their church while the children stayed in day care at the Social Services Center. "Fortunately, with the help of social security benefits and food stamps, I was able to afford a one bedroom apartment and pay bills." She paused, and once again her pleasant demeanor returned. "Take a walk through the house and see if you like what I've done with it. I'll prepare sandwiches and drinks for our lunch."

The home was simply furnished but immaculate. There were a few pieces of familiar old furniture still in the house. Jane said she had painted them over, herself.

She served them an elegant lunch—elegant more in the manner in which it was served, then in the content—certainly not lavish and expensive, but adequate. Their kids all played happily together, acting as though they were all family.

It turned out to be a wonderful, fulfilling day, something very much unexpected by Danny and Sheila. They made promises to stay in touch.

Before leaving, everyone gathered together in a semi-circle in front of Grampa's portrait; the spouses, the children, all of them. For a few long moments, no one spoke or made a sound. Sheila wiped away a few tears. Jane held her daughter Melissa in her arms. The child broke the silence as she took her thumb from her mouth and pointed at the painting and in her little voice said, "Grampa." The mother's face reddened. "I...I told the children it was their grandfather's picture." She hesitated. "I thought it would be nice for them to have a grandfather." She quickly added, "I have an old blanket that you can wrap the picture in to take with you."

Sheila motioned to Danny and they stepped aside and whispered to each other.

Sheila turned to Jane. "Danny and I think Grampa's portrait should stay right there over the fireplace. That's where it belongs. Where Mom wanted it to be when this was their house." She paused to wipe tears from her eyes. "We're sure of that."

On the way home in the car, they all marveled at how something that once had seemed so terrible, could have turned into something so good. They recalled Grampa would often say after Ma died, she was still guiding him from up above and as usual, making sure he always did the right thing.

It seems he was right.

THE END

About the Author

Vincent "Vince" D'Angelo

Vincent "Vince" D'Angelo, is a former developer and entrepreneur in the New York City suburbs. He also did freelance writing for building and aviation publications. Upon retirement, he devoted time to writing fiction, plays and screenplays. Writing is a great form of pleasure to him.

The play form of "Being of Sound Mind and Body" was selected a few years ago as one of the award winners of Naples' Sugden Theatre's Readers Theater plays and was performed in their Tobye Theatre. It was followed a few years later with an honorable mention for a comedic play titled, "Throw Papa From The Plane".

He presently has two novels available on Amazon, "No-Name Island" and "Forever is Tomorrow" with a third *Out of Hong Kong* soon to be published. All have a basis in his experiences while in the U.S. Navy. He categorizes them as Adventure and Romance novels.

MANDATORY EVACUATION

Pauline Hayton

April 21, 2017

A man was burned today, serious burns requiring an air lift to the Tampa Burns Unit. In an attempt to protect Ngala, his wildlife preserve, Donovan Smith had been using a hosepipe against the seventy-foot flames of a Golden Gates Estates fire that sprang up next to Everglades Boulevard. He faced down hot flames devouring the surrounding brush and trees to save the exotic animals he loved—panthers, rhinoceros, camel, giraffe—and was seriously burned in the process.

With ash raining down on our house, we turned on my daughter's television. The reporter was interviewing a distraught young man who had been trying to save at least one tractor from his father's destroyed farm, wanting to grab something with which to make a fresh start after all was lost.

I glimpsed fellow author Nick Kalvin who lived nearer to the fire than we did. He was being interviewed outside Golden Gate Community Center, a place of respite for displaced residents from the Estates.

Frequent fiery images flashed onto the screen, frightening infernos incinerating homes and sabal palms, Florida's state tree.

The day had started normally. Peter, my husband, was not working at his part-time driving job. We were in the throes of preparing for a house remodel—kitchen and bathroom updates, with a new tile floor throughout. I had been sorting through closets and had amassed a small mountain of goodies to be taken to our favorite thrift store on 10th Street. We loaded up the Highlander, deciding to call in at the tile shop to see if we could find anything we both liked, an almost impossible task for two people with totally opposite tastes in décor.

After the previous day's heavy lifting and moving furniture into the garage, Friday 21st was going to be a light day. As is so often the case, all good plans are easily scuppered. Owing to illness, the tile shop was grossly understaffed so after a quick inspection we left to deliver our treasures at the thrift store and find a place for lunch. Driving north on US 41 in a choking smoke-haze with ash falling like black snowflakes, we figured there must be another brush fire somewhere in Collier County, not to mention the recent first serious brush fire in Big Cypress Reserve.

Hunger satisfied with a hearty steak and salad followed by ice cream, we headed home east along Pine Ridge Road. Florida Highway Patrol and sheriff deputies speeding past us with lights flashing had us wondering if there had been an accident ahead. But there had been no accident. On reaching Collier Boulevard, it looked like there had been a massive prison break or that serious offenders had been rampaging through our corner of Naples. Law enforcement presence was flooding the area, every corner marked with blue and red flashing lights, with helicopters overhead.

Wondering what was going on, we turned into our mile-long, dead-end street. Police vehicles were going up and down the street. Heck, there were even numerous sheriff's deputies on foot, getting hot and sweaty going up the long drives in the heat, to knock on residents' doors.

Mandatory evacuation they told us.

What? Us?

Twenty-five years living in this street and nothing like this had happened before. There had been that incident when the SWAT team was dealing with a dangerous stand-off in a domestic situation near the entrance to the street. I had been attending classes five nights a week, 6-10 pm., for several months, training to be a massage therapist. Only this particular night, the night of the SWAT team action, my instructor had been suffering with a blinding migraine. "Would you mind if we finished class early? I don't think I can teach you tonight."

Would we mind? Hell no! People were charging out of the room. We had been in class five nights a week, away from our loved ones for what seemed like forever. Polite students commiserated with our instructor and hoped he would soon feel better before galloping off home to spend a bonus evening with their partners.

I arrived at the end of my street to find it blocked by SWAT and no access allowed. What a disappointment. My neighbors and I languished for three hours at the entrance until, at midnight, someone took pity on us and allowed us to drive past the drama one vehicle at a time.

The state trooper at our door mopped his perspiring brow. "We can't force you to leave, but it would be wise. The fire is growing. The wind is pushing it this way and it's only 10% contained."

A picture of my sister flashed to my mind. While we had emigrated from England to Florida, she had immigrated to Perth, Western Australia. She had told me how she and my brother-in-law, when in their late sixties, had used hoses to successfully fight off a brush fire in defense of their home. I had called her all the silly devils in the world for being so fool-hardy.

Now the question was: Should we stay and be prepared to use hosepipes?

Peter insisted we leave.

The light flashed red on the answering machine (no cell phone service at our house.) There were six messages from concerned granddaughters and daughter worried for our safety. It was nice to know they cared.

I phoned my daughter and arranged to stay with her in a safe area of town. A few hours later, one of my granddaughters had to take refuge there too.

We had five cats, three older savvy cats that mainly lived outdoors, and two one-year-olds who were innocents. We scooped the youngsters into carry cases. The other three were nowhere to be found. We put out lots of dry food and water for them and threw cat food for the young cats into a bag.

We gathered together insurance policies, pension plan information, passports and e-tickets for our planned trip to England and India in the fall. I grabbed my computer, containing all the details of our lives and years of my writing and put it into the back of the Highlander. I racked my brains for what else I should take—all my notes for books I was writing or intended to write, two large boxes of them; tax documents, photographs of past generations of family; pictures of the Indian villagers and pupils we had grown to love from our sponsorship of their village school; photos of our belongings.

Tom, our neighbor strolled over as we locked up. "Leaving?"

"Yes. You?"

"Nah. I'm staying. Gonna guard my place from thieves with my gun."

I didn't doubt it. Peter had come face-to-face with Tom's gun when he was searching outside one night for one of our cats that had been missing a couple of days.

Looking back as we drove down the drive, I noticed our normally shiny metal roof was dull grey from all the ash covering it. Fingers crossed everything would still be standing in a day or two. If not, our home insurance would be paying for the new kitchen and bathrooms we had planned and we would save a stash of money.

At my daughter Jackie's house, we settled in as best we could. Jackie was tired from a long day at work and my son-in-law Gordon had been up since 4:00 am. for work. Peter and I tossed all night, worried about our three cats left behind. We brought Henry and Roscoe, our two young cats, into the bedroom for the night because they were so unsettled by the changes. They disturbed us by seeking attention and reassurance. All our cats were starving strays who found their way to our house during the recession. Henry we found as a ten-week old kitten by the roadside one dark morning. To say we are protective, and perhaps over the top regarding their welfare, could be considered an understatement.

Next morning, we returned home to check on the cats fending for themselves. They were perfectly safe. Rain was expected later in the day and we hoped to return then if it was heavy enough to dampen the fire.

At Jackie's, we passed the time playing cards while waiting for the rain to come. As predicted by weather forecasters, it fell like manna from heaven at 3:00 pm. First, just a few spaced out rings on the surface of the lake outside the window. It faded, stopped. Hearts sank. Then came another surge of raindrops hitting the lake's surface. With rings galore covering the lake from end to end, the shower turned into a downpour. I was truly grateful and hoped no one else would lose their home or be hurt by the fire. It was time to return home.

We were the fortunate ones. Our house and animals were unscathed. But we have learned an important lesson. Unlike approaching hurricanes, when we receive plenty of advance warning, fires can flare up suddenly and travel fast, quickly putting residents in the danger zone. Be prepared to flee at a moment's notice. Prepare your list of important documents and belongings to snatch up and run.

THE END

86

About the Author
Pauline Hayton

From the northeast of England, Hayton worked twelve years as a probation officer in her hometown of Middlesbrough before immigrating to the United States in 1991 with her husband Peter. They live in Naples, Florida, willing slaves to their five adopted cats.

Hayton never harbored dreams of becoming a writer, but after listening to her father's war stories and reading his tattered wartime diaries, she felt compelled to write his WWII memoir *A Corporal's War*. Several books and magazine articles followed.

Stumbling upon Ursula Graham Bower's story, the author knew instantly that she would write a book about this extraordinary woman. *Naga Queen* is a biographical fiction based on eight years in Ursula Graham Bower's life, set in India during WWII.

Having twice survived cancer, the author celebrated by going to Myanmar (Burma) to follow in her father's WWII footsteps. She made a documentary film of the trip for her grandchildren and wrote a travelogue of the trip.

Chasing Brenda, 2012, is a comedy adventure novella based on Hayton's first visit to a remote village in NE India.

Published in 2013, *If You Love Me, Kill Me* is a novella based on the author's personal experience of caring for her elderly parents.

Hayton's latest books are her inspirational life story *Still Pedaling* and her first children's book *The Unfriendly Bee*.

When the door to writing opened, I stepped through and followed the unfurling path. It changed my life. As a result of writing *Naga Queen*, my husband and I became sponsors of Mt. Kisha English School where our efforts educate the more than 100 Naga children in Magulong village, NE India, an experience that enriches our retirement years.

Books available in paperback and kindle.

Author Websites: www.paulinehaytonauthor.com
www.amazon.com/author/paulinehayton

LOST AT THE BEACH

CHAPTER ONE

Nick Kalvin, MD ©

In the dark and rain, Louie searched frantically in a zigzag pattern. Used a small red-lens battery lantern close to the sand. *This weirdo job! Shit! No luck... Should have known! No prelims, no scouting the mark! A fool's errand from the get-go.*

Now, getting close to sunrise, forced to go back, retrace steps, looking for a damn rental car key! At least, I'm probably, still the only living person out here.

He'd accepted this contract, thinking it would be his last. Ten years ago, he purchased a hill-side lot in Stella Maris, a nice, quiet development. For almost sixty years, it spanned the upper portion of Long Island in the Bahamas. His retirement cottage, near the top of the uniquely high and long limestone ridge, faced west to the Caribbean. Only miles wide, Long Island was ninety miles in length. Unlike other Bahama islands, it featured a long, rocky spine. Took two years to complete his neat, retirement home. Most of one dry season lost when a wicked hurricane damaged the little harbor and slowed local businesses to a crawl.

At last, with thick, cool rock walls, a rain-catching, white roof, a large cistern, parking and storage under the floor, a patio lush with mango, orange, lemon, lime, grapefruit, fig, guava, banana and star-fruit trees, it was his bit of paradise.

Last month, after buying himself two fine, official Cuban Maduro cigars at the Stella Maris Inn bar, he walked back to his haven. Stayed up all night. Watched the moon traverse the semi-tropical sky. Leisurely smoked and sipped iced bourbon in his hammock. Looked up into endless space. There was a sweet aroma of Grapefruit, Key Limes and Valencia blossoms emanating from his bricked patio. He felt at peace. It was time to hang it up. Watched countless stars. Identified slowly rotating constellations. Gazed at the moon, until the Eastern sky turned pink.

A week later, in a decrepit Brooklyn neighborhood deli, his agent offered one last job. Louie grimaced, but said, "I accept, Max. But, after that, man, I aim to disappear. Never come back." Louie stuffed instructions, maps and a wad of cash inside his security pocket of his worn but comfortable, concealed carry travel jacket. As he drove away, he pictured himself fishing, diving, drinking, relaxing, finally reading his way through the stacks of books, back at Stella Maris. Each time he visited he brought another carton of them for his bookcases, which lined the two longest walls. Salvaged from flea markets and dusty used-book stores all over the US and Canada.

Louie always enjoyed reading, but hid any taste for it, as far back as 6th grade. Had several hundred more books of all types, sorted, boxed in a secret Miami air conditioned storage unit, along with his tools of trade.

Tonight, on this last job, carefully re-tracing his path to the target's beach, he wanted this ugly task done. *Shit! Wish I never heard of it.* With several numbered accounts around the globe, he could be free for the rest of his life. Instead, he might be jinxed, apprehended, finished by daylight. Instead of being miles away, he was forced to waste time, take a huge risk going back to the scene.

Instead, for the first time, since his first intentional hit, he was way beyond nervous. He could end up in some dirty Florida prison cell, just around time's corner, instead of his Caribbean paradise.

His stomach cramped. Sweat oozed beneath his hooded raincoat, got in his eyes. He blinked. *Damn dawn approaching. Soon be here. The target was where it was said to be. But, my God, what a shock that turned out to be.* The steady rain slowed to a cool drizzle. He sighed. *Not a soul in sight. No car key so far. Certainly, not in the grass around the parking area, nor on the footpath through the dunes.*

Louie was a fiercely careful professional, with a perfect record. Indirectly bought by some of the highest paying anonymous clients in the Hemisphere. His last few fees totaled more than he could count as a little kid in Cleveland. His father still ran that run-down, tile-floored deli in a now tough, mixed-race part of the city, which abutted a large public park. During his young years, it was a safe, cozy, mixed Lower European neighborhood. Contact with his family became rare, due to his trade.

The fall prior to sixth grade, he was ordered to wear Dad's Sunday trousers and shirts to school. Once Louie became the old man's size, Mom and Dad quit buying him new things, to be able to afford clothes for his four sisters. Unfortunately for Louie, this came during the very period when pre-teens became fashion and fad conscious.

Other guys quit teasing him about his odd, old-country, ill-fitting wardrobe, once they tasted his knuckles and damaged brand-new, teen-fad garb with their own blood. Girls continued to tease, point, and giggle behind his back in the halls, or when he was surrounded by them, at his locker. One pretty thing advised, "Louie, Louie! Why don't you start wearing suspenders? Take up some of that excess cloth! It sags below your ass!" Her posse, confident he would not hurt females, giggled at his discomfort.

Red-faced, he'd muttered, "Stupid bitches, fuck you all." They laughed louder.

Intelligent, perceptive, clever, he grew suspicious of and disliked most students. In high school, he changed resentments to aggression, a desire to punish unlucky swells from the suburbs on football fields and wrestling mats. He almost upset one such, Mr. Cleveland, a flashy body-builder from Tech High, ranked second in the state in 165-pound class. Got a takedown and a near-fall in the opening period but, was pinned himself, in the last few seconds of a long, tough-fought match with a strange maneuver which he never saw before, despite observing hundreds of matches.

Beyond sports, it was hard for him to obey school rules. At times, school ended in detention which was held in woodshop, after the final bell. The administration thought that was a tough corrective measure. But, "detent" was nothing compared to what waited after school, when he showed up late at the deli.

No sense trying to explain or duck the blows. Heavy, ham-handed slaps to the sides of his face and head, by his red-faced, disappointed father. In his father's defense, he cheerfully forgave lateness and absence, if it was for scheduled sport events. More than once, he apologized for never coming to after-school wrestling, football games and other events. Said he wished he could be there to see Louie out there. One time he hugged Louie long and apologetically, saying in Italian, "Son, if only I didn't have so many damn bills to pay, I would be there every time." Pops kissed his own medallion. "I swear it on my patron saint."

Deli duties included: besides cleaning up the small toilet, sweeping the sidewalk, steps, entrance, then the entire store floor, restocking cans, boxes, bottles, produce, re-hanging meats in the cold room, taking out the trash, taking apart and cleaning the antique coffee grinder, and setting out empty bottles in proper crates for deposit returns. Then make a few grocery bag deliveries on his way home to supper. Poppa remained until 9 PM for after-work and evening shoppers: Deli sandwiches to-order, warm-up-and-eat pasta cartons, selling paper cups of Italian Ice, Gelati from Tuscany, American-made chocolate drumsticks, soft drinks, bottled beers from Genoa and Sicily.

Yep, Pops was painfully honest, hard-working, hard-nosed but, short-fused. His thick fingers and calloused hands smelled of meat, garlic, sausages and seasonings. Delivered stunning open-hands which would floor a weaker kid. Days he arrived late after detention afternoons, Louie blinked away flashing lights in his head which lingered after the slaps. The old man, if provoked to use his fists, had cold-cocked some bigger men, toughest dudes in the several-block area. Once at the annual church picnic at Purita Springs Amusement Park, right in front of the parish priest.

After the slaps, Pop, beet-red in the face, garlic breathed, always yelled, "Now, first, clean the God damn toilet, then do your other jobs!"

Louie's cauliflower ears came not from wrestling or boxing, but from Papa's crackling smacks. A week before his junior year, Louie argued with line-backers coach, one hot-as-Hell August day. It was Monday. Football's first two-a-day.

Louie worked most of a late summer weekend helping his father clean and repaint the entire store, moving heavy cabinets, refrigerators, barrels of goods. Then spent Saturday and Sunday evenings setting pins at the bowling alley until midnight for pocket cash. Come Monday morning, as the sun rose, Louie was gassed. After a solid hour of vigorous routines, Head Coach, noticed Louie's performance. He marched over. Called Louie a lazy backslider in front of the team. Louie threw his scarred helmet, which bounced off the scraggly turf to hit an assistant coach in a knee. Flustered, Louie left the practice field. Even bumped into and swore at the unexpecting high school disciplinarian, the Dean of men, who had also come in before classes, but took a break before lunch, to watch practice.

Louie never returned to the team. He found out years later, that his coaches considered him two-sport college material. A scout, an AD assistant from Ohio State had come to that practice session to look at several boys from last fall's conference champs, including Louie. It wasn't until the tenth team and class reunion that Ray Jackson, the black fullback, told Louie what the head coach told assistants that day Louie stomped off the practice field. No one heard but Ray and the quarterback, who both ended up standing closest to the coaches and the young man from Columbus. "Screw Louie! That hot-headed bastard! Just fucked up his future, lost a chance to be a Buckeye! And, after all we've done to help him get his head on straight. Tough shit! Let him go."

Ray won a full ride to Syracuse, including a two year post grad scholarship in the Arts. He blocked for Jaxon Jefferson, the all-American running back. Ray gave Louie a beer and told him about those after-practice remarks. Louie thanked Ray and clinked bottle necks. In his heart, Louie knew as a kid, he was tough, talented, and effective. But, like other grunts, felt neglected as the same coach tolerated real goof-offs, sass, bullshit, free-styling, instead of running plays as diagramed, from elite athletes. Even let one player, who had missed a final, pre-game practice. But, that was the world. Kids like Louie were not blind. Nor were they happy about the double standards.

The ordinary boys, black, white, Latin even the rare Asian or Jewish kid, had to toe the line, show up each day, give it all in practice, wind-sprints, prolonged jump squats, tackling, blocking, pushing that rusting sled with a couple of fat coaches on it to the point of vomiting. In those days, a boy was regarded as a pussy if he wanted water during practice. In that era, coaches, unaware of heat stroke and perspiration dehydration, ridiculed those who passed out.

Next day, Louie took the street car downtown instead of school. He enlisted in the Marines. He learned quickly. Became a sniper, loved the tactical stuff, weapons, scouting, patrols and shooting. But a Navy shrink asked Louie to describe some blots of ink, then disqualified his application for the Navy Seals. As a result, Louie had some drunken liberties, flare-ups with squad mates and an NCO. Just short of two years active duty, he was discharged as "unsuitable."

Instead of going home, he moved in with an old teammate, a former defensive tackle, Zeke Zalinski. In high school, Zeke made loans to buddies. Never was short of school lunch or snack cash. He ran campus football pools and numbers for a connected uncle. After graduation, Zeke joined the outfit. Climbed the local mob ladder. Stayed handsome. Flashy dresser, with lots of girlfriends. Zeke introduced Louie to the outfit.

In Zeke's environment, Louie was discrete, grateful, gained respect as dependable, well trained, and unshakeable. He rose through ranks: running errands, cash pick-ups, keeping an eye out for the fuzz, scouting marks, became a courier trusted with bulky, graft envelopes to cooperative cops and city officials, then, assistant debt collector, head leg-breaking collector, and finally was promoted to the Capo's personal body guard and special functions unit.

Always available, never complained, or questioned orders. Promptly completed each job. Two years later,

Capo took him to a fancy Italian restaurant in Shaker Heights. After an elegant Tuscan meal, several courses with wines for each, Capo folded his linen napkin. He leaned over a silver tray of cut fruit, cheeses and the small pot of espresso. Capo grasped one of Louie's jacket lapels. In a whisper, he said, "Lou, I'm going to recommend you to an agent for a group of contractors. This is a great opportunity, son. You will be an independent man. A wealthy one if you're careful." Capo tapped Louie's temple. "Up here, you got what it takes."

In this new line of work, Louie fell back on military training. He loved the job. Time between contracts allowed him lots of freedom to travel and be alone. His assignments required patience, ingenuity, good surveillance, risk assessment, secrecy, contingency plans, two or more escape plans, considering everything that might happen. Weather, light, other people, breaks in the target's routine and habits. Each contract meant cash, lots of cash. He was no longer required to hang out making idle chat at some smelly mob bar-and-grill, or stale billiard hall, awaiting orders, then breaking fingers, cracking knees to collect bad debts and unpaid bets. He did not have to be a toady in the Capo's crew, keeping watch outside some house or apartment all night, while the made-men screwed mistresses or enjoyed all-night poker sessions.

Louie never knew who or what mob or family hired him, or why. He just took the order. Carried it out. He was very good, very careful. Soon did a dozen jobs a year, each worth several thousands in crisp bills. That was when five G per year was considered good pay for teachers. Capo was right. Louie became an independent.

He lost weight, turned clean-shaven, polite, quiet, un-noticed, dressed like a business executive, careful in planning and surveillance. Cool in the moment. He smoothly defused confusion or neutralized rare hints of alarm with an innocent remark until it was too late for the target. Most marks never knew what was coming. A few had seconds to realize they'd been fingered. Surprised, open-mouthed, with no time to utter a word.

Most of them deserved what they got anyway. From the contract info, his studies and prep time, he knew more about them than wives and mothers. Most were snitches, CFIs, creeps and skimmers. Some were real assholes. Slimy child molesters, serial rapists or wife beaters. Louie was certain those contracts were bought by enraged parents, maybe even by an occasional detective, DA or pissed off prosecutor unable to convict an escape-artist pervert. Some by a battered wife or girlfriend, who finally had enough. He enjoyed those jobs immensely. Made sure he arranged for opportunity, isolated location and time. Unlike the average hit, he slowed things down, leisurely allowed maximum awareness, and as much suffering as could be dished out. Those hits, Louie felt like he was taking out garbage. For them, his gun was far too merciful.

Yeah, targets generally got what they deserved . . . a few were wild, crazy assholes who, despite good advice, persisted in drawing undue attention to some mob. A small percentage seemed to be clean-record folks. Trial witnesses or even ordinary Joes? Fears of conviction, anger at betrayal, jealousy, revenge or affairs likely triggered those deals.

With no clues or prep, this job seemed weird from the day he accepted it. Louie was only told to be on this shitty, rainy beach at 4 AM, this morning. That the target would be the only person there. "No prep or scouting necessary. In and out. See Marco Island, preferably at night. Then, scoot."

So, Louie had just been out on this beach, in dark, drizzly pre-dawn. Luckily, his night vision was excellent. The almanac was right. No moon, but it hadn't mentioned fog and rain. Rain was good, made it even less likely that there'd be unexpected company. So far, just gulls sleeping, a few of them scattered about the sloping sand. Then, he saw a figure ahead, in the drizzle and dark.

Had to be the target! Bent over, holding a red-lens flashlight to the ground, its back to him. Wearing a yellow slicker. Without a sound, Louie closed the distance. He heard a repeated clicking sound as he crept closer. *Too light a noise, too frequent for a weapon. Too quiet for machinery? Hopefully, not a gun.*

Am I the real target? Is this, literally, my last job? Maybe that friggin' agent blabbed that I was quitting business. Someone wants loose ends tied up. Forever. Maybe this target is a reverse set-up, with another contractor to take me out!

Surf noise and increasing rain muffled his last steps. *Very near now.* He held his breath. Slowly raised his cocked pistol fitted with a silencer. *Take no chances. One more step.* Suddenly, a sea shell cracked under his boot. The target whirled around. The yellow raincoat parka top fell away. *Jesus!* He was staring at a marvelously beautiful woman, late twenties. Shocked, she dropped her red-beam flashlight. He glanced down. There were little turtles and broken shells around her feet.

Holy Christ! He'd never offed a dame before! Her frightened eyes flashed. They locked on his. Her soft lips parted. She raised her right hand to her mouth.

Before she could scream or react, his training and preparation kicked in.

He pulled the trigger. There was a blossom of blood and ragged skin, center-hit, middle of her forehead. She fell toward him. With a convulsive movement, she clutched his black Scottish raincoat. He moved back. There was a ripping sound as she fell, face down, to the sand. He grimaced. Shook his head. Stepped to her side. Put another hollow-point, soft lead slug into the back of her skull. He looked around, then turned and rapidly strode back to the parking area.

Sweet baby Jesus! She was counting baby turtles! How harmful could she be to anybody? Dear God, what have I just done? His heart was beating at a fantastic rate. He could hear it pulsing in his ears. First time, after a completion.

It didn't take long to cover the three-football-field distance to the unassuming grey, rental sedan. With a sigh, he leaned against the left fender, stunned. *I just killed a real looker. More beautiful than any Victoria Secret model or Playboy Bunny. Who the hell would want her dead? Money problems, divorce, jealous lover?*

He sagged under an immense weight of sadness, shame and regret. *Not only beautiful, but with smarts. And sympathy enough to care about even the damn baby turtles. So unlike those stuck-up, phony bitches, who'd populated old Cleveland parochial and public schools.* He swore.

His heart ached. He'd been hoping to find a female like the target since he was thirteen. Suddenly, his mouth filled with sour saliva and his stomach clenched. He bent over. For the first time after a job, Louie puked. On the car, his boots and the grassy dune. He needed a drink. He grabbed his thermos on the front seat, rinsed his mouth with still hot black coffee. Shivering and sweating at the same time, he twisted off the silencer. Put his gun into his right-side pocket. Then, he reached for the tagged rental key fob deep in his left raincoat pocket.

What the fuck? Groped for the key, his left hand came out through the torn inside bottom of the left side pocket. *Holy shit! The seam's pulled apart at the bottom. Key's lost somewhere. Mother fucker!*

Slow down. Breathe. He picked up the small battery lantern he left on dim, just under the driver's door. Turning it to bright red light, he searched around the car. *No key, just chunks of Waffle House eggs and bacon, black coffee, stomach acid mixed in the grass. Got to go back, retrace. Go!* He quickly stepped, side-to-side, back and forth, scout-style, lantern low to ground, frantically looking.

Soon, he was back on the still dark beach, a faint glow low on the Eastern horizon. *Daylight on the way. Not much time. No other place for the key to be. Likely near her right hand which grabbed at the left side of his expensive hooded coat.*

Back at the body, he looked. *Shit!* No key on ground, nor in her right or left hand.

He saw a huge, square-cut diamond on her left ring finger. . . *Engaged! Fuck it!*

"Sorry, honey," he whispered. Gently rolled her over onto her back. Her face, was still lovely despite a dusting with sticky grains of bloody sand. Open, staring turquoise eyes, pale lips apart. Pupils wide and still. Very little outside bleeding. *There! Where she molded the wet sand.* His key was pressed into it among broken egg shells, her counting device and one dead baby turtle. The poor little thing, next to her flashlight, had been caught, trapped under her chest. The rest, counted and uncounted, had fled.

Briefly, he stared at the victim. *My God, Sweetie, who would ever want you dead?*

He made it back to the car. Got out a large beach towel. Mopped vomit from his boots, the car and the soil. Rinsed residue into the dirt with three jugs of water from the trunk. Carefully, he put the rolled-up soiled towel into a plastic garbage bag, destined for a waste can far away. Got into the car. Checked his gloves for blood and puke. None. He keyed it. Without lights, made a careful, slow drive across south beach parking and access path. He left them off until he saw the big beach hotels and lit crosswalks ahead. He steered north on the still deserted main street, through town, then over the big bridge. North of the island, it was still purplish dark as he motored through the quiet marshlands. He headed for the mainland and US 41 North, to go through Naples. Change of plans. The alternate route to I-75.

His police scanner warned him of a wreck on 951 or South Collier Boulevard, two miles north of 41, east of Naples Lely. He calmed down and cruised under the limit through "The Town on the Trail." At Vanderbilt he turned east, away from the beach area. He chose Vanderbilt over Immokalee and Pine Ridge, as he knew from a previous job, it was less used, darker, with very few stop lights or businesses, much of it woods, entry gates, trees, shrubbery, concrete walls. At Collier Boulevard, 951, he turned right to go south, catch I-75 back to the East coast.

He'd avoid the need to pass a line of cop cars, fire and rescue folks or get held up in stopped traffic down on south 951. The horizon was a pink strip, as he approached Golden Gate Parkway. Near the southwest corner sat a Highway Patrol car. Louie held his breath as he passed by, not too fast, not too slow. He could see a glow in the cop-car from the computer screen. He, the cop, only one at the intersection. Nervously, Louie eyed behind, in his mirrors. But, the cop got a green light, slowly rolled out, did a left to go back north.

Louie liked the Naples area. Somewhere, off Livingston in north Collier County, years ago, Louie attended a mobster's wedding. *A place called Mediterra. Great club house, nice homes, landscape and golf course. One hell of a party.* Once he got on I-75, it should be smooth going. Then, south into Miami, to the Hotel Chateau Bleu, just south of Miami Airport. Louie got out his sunglasses to be ready when the sun came up. He would have an hour or more to think about what had just happened. *That fantastically beautiful and obviously kind woman! Lord!* He turned the scanner off.

Time to think things over. He'd have time on 75. After, he planned some sleep. A good meal in the Greek dining room. The Bleu was a small, nice, quiet, early 1900s era place. A slow, creaky elevator. No A/C in the halls. A casual staff and lots of foreign visitors, who respected privacy. He used it when in Miami. Just off LeJeune Road, he could walk to fine eating places, bars, browse nice shops, enjoy Cuban coffee and pastry. He spent quiet nights there, just outside his room on a private little balcony, sitting in a lounge chair, smoking, with iced vodka or bourbon and a good paperback.

Like others, Bleu was officially non-smoking, but each room had a balcony with an ashtray. Nobody got their jock in a bind if you enjoyed a decent cigar or a coffin nail on your own balcony. Or even down outside at the small pool, with a Cañone, or rich black Onyx and espresso. Tomorrow he'd check out, carefully clean, vacuum, detail his rental, with a special-mix spray, do the outside at a carwash, turn it in and take a cab to Homestead. There he would board a small two-engine plane out on Vic's farm. Take off before next sundown. Vic would land on the little Stella Maris strip. Just 100 yards downhill from his cottage, an easy walk. Vic would go back before dawn.

What the fuck? Up ahead, just north of the Cracker Barrel Restaurant, there were flashing blue and red lights slowing to a stop . . . *a wreck on I-75 east bound ramp!* He slowed down, tried not to look at the deputy, standing with a flashlight, waving him off the left turn, back towards the center lane. He slowed, drove by on 951 south, headed down to Highway 41, the Tamiami Trail. *I'm completing the circumference of a huge circle, getting nowhere fast.* Ironically, near to 41, the first accident, at the two-mile spot, was cleaned up. He made the turn to Miami.

For the first time in years, he thought of his late mother, his four sisters. He recalled his old parish priest, Father Joe Povachesky. His tours of duty as an altar boy,

101

at Sunday mass, and sad Saturday funerals. He rubbed his chin, blinked tears from his eyes. For the first time in 20 years, he felt an honest need for confession. *Maybe later. God knows there's lots to confess. Getting light. Been on road almost three hours.* As he drove into West Miami, he suddenly heard a voice say something, right in his ear. Startled, he quickly stole a look into the back seat. Almost hit a car cutting in front of him, near the Casino. He swore at the careless asshole. *Christ! What a terrible morning, almost FUBAR, (fucked up beyond all recognition), as old Sarge would say.*

Louie missed the old Jarhead. He realized, too late, the bastard was just teaching loyalty, teamwork, putting the mission first, but also, providing skills and experience to do jobs, survive in a crazy, dangerous world, then make it back alive. *He only meant well for dumb, tough young jerks, like me.* Louie left Calle Ocho. Drove up the curved North-bound ramp onto the Palmetto Expressway. He began to see planes from the West coming into Miami International, with the sun rising on the opposite side of the field. *Got to be tough on pilot vision.* He turned right onto the Airport Expressway, east. Put on his aviator sunglasses.

What the fuck? Again, Louie swore he heard someone talking to him, in the car, empty, except for him. *What was it that the voice said? I must be cracking up at last. Really time to quit.* From the airport expressway, he turned south onto Lejeune Road. *Pay attention, shit head! Don't have an accident for Christ's sake. Morning traffic picking up, early commuters and trucks.*

Suddenly, that voice was more discernible, unmistakably female. It said, "Louie, it's me. I'm going to be alright. I forgive you for shooting me. It was just business, as they say. But, now, Louie I want you to get the SOB who bought you. Do it. I am going to bug you. Hound you. Haunt you till it's done. Then, I'll do my very best to see that you are forgiven, at least for me. Believe me. I'm a great attorney. Or, better say, I was one." Startled, frightened, Louie almost hit a pedestrian stepping off the curb by the Bleu's front door.

He pulled in by the back door and pool. Parked. Got out. Looked in the backseat and trunk. *Empty except for my stuff.* He was wet with sweat. His mouth dry as sand. *God, I need a double vodka and some sleep!*

THE END

RANDOMIZED SCIENCE FICTION

Nick Kalvin, M.D. ©

Abe Brouillard, a retired science fiction writer, lived quietly. After reading the local Sunday edition, he and wife, Alexis, normally walked the Gulf Shore near their condo-tower home. When Abe, at last, put his favorite section down, she looked up from her New York Times crossword puzzle. This morning she surprised him at breakfast. Asked if he wanted to attend church for a change, instead. He laughed at her suggestion, but did not say, yes or no. So, she smiled at him.

As he prepared the NDN for the recycle bin, she said, "You didn't give me a definite answer about attending service."

"Alexis, why on earth would we do that? To me, the only significant time we went to church was to get married. And we did that to keep our parents happy. We should include when we had the kids baptized, went to First Communions, Christmas and Easter pageants. Then there are all the times I dropped you and the girls off for Sunday School and Mass, when they were still young. Why now, Honey?"

She shrugged. Took a sip from her second cup of coffee and said, "Gee, I just had this feeling we should. After all, it's a gorgeous Sunday morning and we have so much to be thankful for. It happens to be Easter morning. It's been so long." She paused and regarded him over the brim of her cup. "Plus, Abe, dear, it's also the six-month anniversary of your heart attack. Seems like yesterday when you told me to fetch Father Michael. Get him to the cardiac care unit, to hear your confession and give you communion. Last rites, if they couldn't stop that arrhythmia. So, once more, what do you think, down deep, about attending services again?"

He grinned, scoffed, "What do I think? For starters, Madame, please, finish your coffee. Maybe after the Easter to-do is over and seasonal crowd is gone. Meantime, I'll check on the cat, then get my flip-flops. Today, let's just do our usual walk, along the water's edge, before it gets too damn hot."

Alexis smiled. "Same old Abe. Sticking with your routine. But, you haven't tuned me out. I'll settle for next Sunday. Church attendance at our age is not such a bad idea, honey."

The once famous author looked up, as he rinsed the cat's water dish at the sink. He said, "Sweetie-Honey, you know I'm not that starry-eyed altar boy you fell in love with long ago. Lord, I've changed a lot. We've seen so much, matured, learned there are worlds beyond man's religions. I've had to learn different areas of science, study other faiths to write my books. What Darwin and the evolutionists came up with, makes perfect sense to me. I don't know if I can swear at this moment that I even believe in a Supreme Being anymore. You know, the one thing the Communists ever said, with which I now agree, is that religion is the opiate of the people. But, even the Commies forgot to include religion as a major cause of most wars going back to antiquity, and unrecorded eras prior to that. Don't think, you've mentioned going to mass ourselves, since the girls went off to college."

She walked across the flat to him, set her cup in the sink then hugged him and kissed his cheek. "Okay, Abe, let's take that walk. I need to look for a few special shells to complete my latest Gulf of Mexico collection. You must admit, it's a particularly lovely Easter morning to look for the rarest ones." She stood beside him as he refilled the cat's food and water dishes.

She had made over one hundred shell collections. Attractively arranged in a large shadow box against royal blue velvet, they retailed for three thousand in several high-end Florida shops and one hotel chain. Abe's stream of auto-deposit royalties decreased, year by year. At least her teacher pension held steady. Friends still suffered, following the real estate mortgage collapse and the post-election stock market plunge. Some lost everything, including IRAs and retirement benefits. A few with old, no longer needed skills took menial jobs. With a hand on his shoulder, she smiled, edged him away from the sink with her hip. After spraying off the breakfast dishes, she put them in the washer.

"Last night, after you fell asleep, I could not. Was wide-eyed for some reason. So, I re-read Genesis. Your Mom's Bible opened upon it when I laid it in my lap. You know, it struck me, Abe, how Doctor Gamoff's theory of the 'Big Bang,' and recent proof of an expanding universe, both paraphrase the opening lines of the Book of Genesis. I know people today scoff at the idea of Creation done in seven days. But, at the beginning, we can assume there was no such thing as time, in a human sense. Right? After all, the earth's rotation, apparent movement of the sun across the sky, and the fraction of our yearly orbit, which became 'a day,' didn't exist either. No one was around to invent months, or years." She shrugged a shoulder, waiting for his reply. He didn't. Just raised his eyebrows.

"Look, Abe, what if a 'day' in Genesis, before humans and the earth came to be, could well be one billion years of our time. Call it a God day. If you consider that premise, Genesis and the theories of evolution, recent calculated age of the universe, known geologic eras, why, they all fit together pretty well."

106

Chuckling, he leaned over and kissed her on the tip of her nose. *Still the smartest cookie in the box.* But, what she said rattled him a little. He said, "Precisely! So, you're proving the Biblical version of Creation to be true, you gorgeous thing. Former high school prom queen, Honor Society, Student Council Officer for four years and, the only repeat president of the Future Teachers of America, as I recall." He grinned, "After all, why not? Go over that Creation idea again."

She saw that her words made an impression, which he turned into a joke. That strong, independent self-assured spirit of his. He used it as a shield as he aged. She looked at him and, with wide open eyes, said, "Back then, folks just tried to guess how it all happened, Abe. Even you must admit, it's amazing, quite awesome, that the ancients did get the Big Bang right. What if a 'God Day' is a billion earthly years? From what I have read about the universe, that simple number seven for actual creation and the rest for development comes out pretty darn close."

Abe shrugged. *What she said makes perfect sense. Twelve to fourteen billion altogether. She always was intuitive, extremely intelligent.*

He looked at her and nodded. "I never thought of it that way, Sweetie. Sometimes, you think too deep at the wrong time. Come on. Let's take that walk."

A half hour later, Alexis was lingering behind him, with her large straw shoulder bag, as she stopped to look for suitable shells. She also paused to speak with other collectors and condo neighbors. Abe looked back to see how far behind him she was. When he turned his head back North, he saw an elderly, dapper man with a trim white beard and an ivory-colored cane, splashing along in the water at the edge of the beach.

He wore a white linen suit. He sported a baby-blue, button-down shirt, open at the neck, topped off with a crisp-looking, yellow, straw hat. Jacket unbuttoned, the old guy ambled along, barefoot, in the shallow water. As they were about to pass each other, the man, who had brand new boat shoes tied together, dangling from one shoulder, tipped his hat and spoke. "Hello, Abe! Goodness, I haven't seen you in decades!"

Abe was surprised, "Good morning to you, Sir. Do we know each other?" I don't recall . . ."

The stranger raised a hand. "Oh, yes, Abe, indeed, yes. I know you well. Been reading your stuff almost 60 years. I recognize your style, content, direction. Also, your strongly stated beliefs in areas beyond your expertise. I can even recite your earliest efforts, if you'd like me to, and, have several hours to stand around out here for the monologue. One could say, I've been peering over your shoulder, for a long time. It was fifth grade, when you first began writing fiction. True? At the other end of your span, I can tell you the topic of next Sunday's Metro column, the text of which, you have yet to begin."

What the *hell?* Now beyond simple suspicion, Abe replied, "Really? You don't have to do that! But, really, I don't recognize you at all." Abe looked right, left and behind to see if anyone noticed this totally weird old fellow.

Alexis talking with several people, showing them her shells. Thankfully, no one else was near to hear this crazy conversation.

"My dear, dear Abe. You used to recognize me." The gent shook his head as if disappointed.

Abe peered closely at the deeply lined face, and friendly creases about the visitor's eyes. Through the straw-hat penumbra shading the stranger's face, Abe suddenly realized that the senior citizen had large black pupils, despite the bright morning sunlight. *That, just shouldn't be!* Ben's muscles tightened. Some began to twitch when he saw countless sparks darting and glittering within those eyes. It was like peering through binoculars at some whirling atomic reaction or a spinning galaxy in one of his novels. Abe felt his heart do a double beat, then another.

"Abe! Please, don't be alarmed," said the old man. "It's not that CCU arrhythmia. Look son, I mean you no harm. Just want to talk a bit. Last week you addressed a student assembly at the local High School. Your subject was random evolution. Many of their parents were fans of yours. Most kids today don't read a lot. But, all of them were impressed after the Principal introduced you. You informed those kids, struggling in a failing system, and speaking as a successful writer. And, ahem, as a man of science that you have concluded that even the advent of life, the development of protoplasm, DNA, mitochondria, enzymes, amino acids, nucleic acids, species, that it is all accidental, meaningless, like Legos or Erector Sets assembling themselves out of materials in the city dump.

"You said all that stuff, including lipids, carbohydrates, all the polysaccharides, peptides, and proteins, too, just happened to hook up in the right manner, sequences, exactly at the right time, the right mix, not considering the obvious, required temperature, gravity, pressure, gaseous mixture, light, radiation, moisture, all also coincidentally and simultaneously available, to allow the reaction to begin, let alone sustain activity to reach completion. Even in a modern lab one needs the right conditions. Heavens, you know that! Then, you compared the universe to an immense clock, alone, ticking away in the vast emptiness of space."

The old guy pointed a finger at Abe. "When some kid doubted you, and shouted, 'Who made the clock?' You replied, 'No one.' Then compared universal creation, evolution, to random writing, with letters falling together to form into random words, the random words into meaningful order, and then into logical sentences, which would then merge into intelligent paragraphs, chapters, and books. Constructions of logical, intelligent grammar, alphabetical correctness and word order totally by accident, you said, not some higher power.

"To justify your statement, you used a hypothetical experiment. You claimed, that given enough time, even a blindfolded, cooperative Chimpanzee, seated at a typewriter, would eventually hit enough of the right keys to write the works of Shakespeare, or the books of the Bible. With a different keyboard, with the proper symbols on the keyboard, you finished by saying, the industrious primate might eventually tap out the equations of Isaac Newton and Albert Einstein. The ape someday would even stumble upon the chemical steps to make plastics, steel, synthetic fabrics! Entirely new materials, if that poor creature was only given enough time."

The old guy shook his head. "Do you know what the mathematical odds of just one such happening is, Abe? The odds, that the ape, or several million successive apes to carry on the task, would be able to do just one of the afore-mentioned, are, actually, so great, they make it impossible, Abe. Even I don't have enough time to stand out here, and utter the figures until after eternity ends." He pointed a finger. "Yes, Abe, it would take longer than eternity. That quote comes from an article to be written this fall, by a clever young lady in India, which will be submitted to a mathematical journal and Scientific American for publication next year."

"You may know math, Sir, but I do believe in random creation and evolutionary change. Material which I used for my address to the students has also, bit by bit, all appeared in my op-ed pieces, and the forwards to my novels," Abe replied. "I use entertainment, science fiction, studded with fact and theory to educate readers and stimulate the thinking process in every reader. I'm an honest writer. I write what I know. I know science."

At first, the Old Man didn't respond. Abe noticed the gent never blinked. Then, Abe saw an especially high wave splash knee high upon the old dude's ice-cream pants cuffs. They remained dry, as rivulets ran back to the waterline. After what seemed like minutes, the visitor said, "Abe, my son. You don't write or speak what is the truth. You just pass on what you have come to believe and have concluded what is, or more accurately said, might be the truth. Somewhere back in your life, you slowly began to close your mind. You pulled down your shutters. You began to ignore your own imagination, suppressed your God-given insight. You quit observing, deducing, and learning. You, for the better part, have quit thinking! Man, you have given up being a student of life. And, what you have come to believe, is not necessarily what is real. Instead of being open and objective, you've become dogmatic and defensive." The old man sighed.

"Who are you?" asked Abe.

"Just an old artist plying my craft, as do you." The crafty old fellow reached out and poked Abe in the chest, twice, "Just like you, I create."

Uneasy, Abe backed up a step. "Just why are you talking to me? Why are you here? Surely not to argue in public."

"I'm here today, to conduct a little experiment, with your help. Abe, you just said, you classify yourself as a man of science, correct? Did you not just define yourself as such to me and to those students, last week, some of whom came looking for inspiration and motivation? Certainly not to hear 'What happens, happens.' Really, Abe?"

Suddenly beginning to sweat, despite clouds obscuring the late morning sun, Abe asked, "What sort of experiment are you planning?"

The old gentleman placed one hand on Abe's left shoulder and leaned in closer, tugging gently with his free hand on Abe's unbuttoned floral shirt, to prevent a backward step.

Tipping his head to allow for the brim of his straw hat, he whispered in Abe's ear. "Fear not. It will only take us thirty seconds of earthly time. Our little test of your chimp hypothesis, why, it will be done, over, before Alexis catches up to you. For this experiment, I am going to place you in my own comfortable chair, before your desk-top PC, but in my workplace. However, I've rearranged the keys of the board to eliminate muscle memory. And, that arrangement will be constantly, randomly changing. Plus, you won't be able to see the keys, as I will change the dioptric power of your corneas, then restore it afterwards. Son, you will be completely safe, comfortable. Any drink, refreshment, and needs will be provided for you, by one of my staff." With a tilt of his head, the old man smiled.

"What you are to do, Abe, your contribution in this test of theory, is to write anything you choose. I will allow you to test your ideas of chance-happening, perfectly random, evolutionary composition. I mean, how often can such an opportunity occur? I am giving you the chance of a lifetime! Pardon, I misspeak. You will have thousands of lifetimes to conduct our little experiment. Yet, Mister Science-Fiction-Mixed-With-Fact Author, I promise to have you right back on this beach in a very short span of earth time. Are you ready to put your money where your mouth is?" The old guy swayed side to side like an enthusiastic coach. "Son, are you ready for a challenge? A wonderful, gallant challenge?"

Abe regarded the grinning, tanned, pompous old fellow. "I think that you, Sir, should think about consulting your personal physician." He turned to leave the old fool.

Abruptly, it became cool. Abe realized that he was in an air-conditioned, pleasant space, seated at a desk. His vision was quite blurry, keeping him from seeing any details. His hands were on a familiar keyboard. In the middle, at the bottom, were paperclips, and ball point pens in the slots. One looked blue, and one was red, as he left them yesterday.

The chair, however, was extremely comfy, just as the old man promised. Somewhere a clock ticked, but only every few seconds. After several such ticks, a mechanical voice announced, not the next minute, but the next year, then, then ten years, then a hundred, then a thousand years . . . on and on. Abe tried to calm his anxiety. Time suddenly seemed important. He frowned, determined to prove the old man wrong.

He realized his mind was filled to overflowing, with all sorts of ideas, some old, most new. His creative urges surged like reined stallions, inspired, spurred by a spinning, rising whirlpool of concepts and realizations. His fingers flew over the keys. He wrote countless columns, articles, short stories, and dozens of poems. He loved it, those poems pulsing from his head down into his fingers. He rocked side to side with the rhythm and rhyme as he typed them out, faster and faster. God! They were great poems. After a hundred, he quit counting them, as more sprouted in his head.

Funny, I always hated poetry before, ever since sixth grade. I'm going to move on, to several new science fiction novels.

The words and chapters poured out. He made outlines for dozens of other books. He wrote five-hundred pages on astrophysics and intergalactic travel. He solved mathematical puzzles which, he knew, had bewildered inventors of the computer, the internet and a host of long-dead, genius mathematicians. His mind raced. He finished with a two-thousand-page trilogy, about galactic wars, expanding universes, parallel universes, universes within molecules of each other, like Russian dolls.

He wrote of future humanoids smart enough to flee erupting suns, by simply shifting their planet into deeper orbit when their own star put out too much radiant heat, and moving the planet back in during periods of low solar radiation production, so the race could survive. One leader wanted an ethical solution. He insisted on saving everyone, to survive without drawing lots to see who would flee by escaping to someplace else, and who, (the majority), would be left behind and barbecued to death.

And Abe could see the means, visualize the forces necessary for planetary manipulation. He could do the calculus to make it work, either way. The last of the three immense books contained a working mathematical hypothesis of what black holes did to light and matter. During that effort, he had another flash of insight. He came up with a relatively easy formula for bending light back the way it came. He grinned.

This may be the way to time travel, forwards and back. Heavens! Really, quite simple. Why hadn't someone thought of it before? I can calculate intra-atomic attractive forces. I see things in several forms, electrical charges and spaces at once. Quantum theory! Wow! Opening one door leads to other doors, and others and others!

He needed a break. He paused. He was thirsty. A blurry figure, in white, placed a goblet in his hand. He drank it, the most refreshing watery liquid he had ever tasted. The goblet seemed to fill, as he drank. His mind was cooling down. His attention focused again on his surroundings. He became aware of the ticking and that robotic clock voice. The voice announced that it was 100,000,000 years since he sat down.

Abe startled and gasped. "What the hell?"

He grabbed both arms of the leather swivel chair, dropping the goblet. There was a tinkling, echoing, prolonged, melodious crash as it hit the hard floor.

Abe tried to see around him, spun in the chair, but his sight was too blurred. The white figure was gone. He shouted, "Hey, Old Man, what's going on?" There was a prolonged, bright white flash and a great whooshing sound.

Suddenly, Abe was squinting up a dazzling blue sky. Sweat popped up from pores on his face. He was lying on the warm beach, feeling Florida's moist spring heat. Despite it, he was shaking, and he had a sense of terrific fatigue. He struggled briefly to sit up. Slowly, he got to his feet. The old man grabbed him.

"There, there, Abe, easy does it." His elderly companion had to support him for a few seconds to steady him.

"What just happened? What did you do to me?" gasped Abe. He tested his arms and legs, rubbed his eyes.

The old gent spoke softly, "Well, our little experiment, which I had described, put you in another dimension, and into an accelerated time system, equivalent to 100,000,000-plus earth years. I let you write to your heart's desire. I gave free rein to your creative urge, your considerable knowledge, insight, skills developed with your own familiar computer. I admit, I had to fiddle around a bit. I had to adjust both you and your computer to allow each of you to last through the entire experiment.

"Those were the conditions to give you a taste of almost an unlimited time, yet preserve you as you are. To allow you to produce meaningful, and wonderful stuff, with your tools of your own trade, in perfect comfort and safety." The old man took hold of Abe's sweaty shirt's lapel. "But, of course, there was a catch. Your own conclusion, that there is only chance in the universe, meant you, yourself, during this time, would be limited to random chance. The constant turnover of the scrambling keyboard, in a non-predicable fashion, did that.

"So, Abe, we put to the test your own belief in random evolutionary creation, and at the same time, your fable about the hypothetical ape with a computer producing Shakespeare's plays, and Isaac Newton's theories. That variable, was my randomizing, rolling, keyboard shuffle.

"We wanted to see, to prove if any of what your brain, far better than any chimp's, might come up with in such a very long time. And to see if those ideas and writings would be able to challenge, penetrate and survive constant randomization. Abe, you ground out much, so much more than I expected. We got a hundred million years' worth of product. I am so proud of you, Son. Indeed, you are a good worker!"

Abe's vision was shifting into focus. He was amazed to see, next to the old man, on the beach, an immense, pearl-colored moving van. Strangely, everyone, who walked by, ignored it, except for a little boy, who seemed about three years old. Beach strollers walked right through it. Holding his bucket and plastic shovel, the kid stood and stared up at the van, shading his eyes with his free hand.

"What the heck is that?" asked Abe. He was feeling somewhat better.

"Why, dear Abe, that van contains all the manuscripts you created, but, of course, limited by chance order of letters, symbols, numbers and punctuation. Simple randomness against of all your intelligence, skills, ideas as a seasoned writer and creator of best-selling print, back in the day. My gift on this day of realization, was to give you a chance to test your hypothesis, to write even that huge Science Fiction trilogy, and so much more, milling around in your brain. You typed tons of stuff. I had to work to cram it all into that van." The old man waved an arm.

"Oh, sorry, Abe. I forgot to say that I took advantage of my position to download calculus, astrophysics, quantum theory and other embellishments, into your cranial matter computer, to further broaden your already remarkable capabilities. I wanted you to have every chance to succeed."

The old man climbed a small ladder into the back of the huge moving van, He held out a hand to help Abe up. The van was packed, floor to ceiling with rubber-banded bundles of printed paper, some in large three-ring, notebooks, still more in stacked folders and boxes. There was a central aisle, but the front wall was too far away, for Abe to see it.

Abe eagerly grabbed a nearby bundle. He pulled off the band, and put on his drugstore reading glasses. Eagerly, he scanned one page after another. Then, he simply flipped the corners, like a large deck of cards. He groaned as he increased his speed of searching. He tossed the ream aside and grabbed another.

He felt his knees weaken. Nothing made any sense. No words. No sentences. Just page after page of scrambled letters, capitals, lower case, numbers, symbols, meaningless spaces and punctuation marks. He dropped that second bundle, spilling the five hundred pages. He went to several more, and tore off the rubber bands. *Same thing in each packet! Just a rambling continuation of meaningless crap!* At this point, he and the old guy stood in a three-foot pile of spilled paper.

The old gentleman spoke, gently. "That's right, Abe, every page in this van is just like that. Nothing produced despite your wonderful, I admit, spectacular, creative urges, inspiration, expanded capabilities and intelligence when limited by a truly random alphabet. How did you ever come to conclude that some happy-go-lucky, hooting and howling primate, slapping random keys, would ever produce anything meaningful? Let alone your SF trilogy, a Shakespearean play, the Bible? To say nothing of complex, insightful, theories and truths about the Universe?"

"But Sir," countered Abe, "we haven't looked at much of what's here. Some of it must contain, at least, a few connected words. Got to be bits of sense which convey some meaning, and function. Let's look at some more. Something must have survived. At least a few words, or isolated threads of thought or purpose, somewhere here. Some phrases, hopefully, a simple sentence. Got to be some, someplace!"

"Abe, my man, Abe," cautioned the old man., "You are a hard case. Okay, Son. Tell you what. When I leave, all these papers, which you typed on your scientific sojourn, will be moved to a storage site right here in Florida, in your town, just for you. Heavens, you can look, read, try to decode, rummage all you want. However, at your age, you won't get through even one or two percent of what's in that van. You have at least a warehouse or two of stuff in there. It reminded me of the loaves and the fishes, only this task was much, much larger." He smiled at Abe and patted his shoulder.

"I think you have better things to do in your remaining years. Heavens! You have people, family, activities, your affairs to look after in the time left to you. Don't waste it. But, I'll leave that choice entirely up to you. That thing called, 'free will,' which you Americans are, so especially, privileged to enjoy."

Abe felt tired. He had a headache. He slumped, head down, and sat on the tailgate of the van. He was a little dizzy. He felt cold on his right palm. The old man was pressing a cold orange juice box into it. He stuck a straw into the box. "Drink, Abe, drink up, your blood sugar is a little low, seventy-five, I believe."

Abe eagerly drank the juice. He handed back the box. "Old man, just who are you?"

The elder man stroked his classic Van Dyke white beard. He brushed some paper shreds from a sleeve. He quickly climbed down the short ladder to the sand. He stood next to Abe's knees. Gently, he tapped on one with a forefinger and said, "Your mother should have named you Thomas, not Abraham."

He tipped his chin up and looked at Abe with a soulful, starry gaze, and shrugged. "Son, I rarely answer that query. You see, I try not to interfere. I have made a point of that. You're a very intelligent fellow, you figure it out. However, I will admit that one of my best students, ever, boldly told a colloquium of theoretical physicists that, I don't, and would not, roll dice. If young Einstein had been at that high school auditorium, he might have booed your chimpanzee experiment example . . . called you out. So long, Abe."

Suddenly, the old man and the huge van were gone. The curious little boy, clearly disappointed, turned and left. His mother watched, with her hands on her hips. He walked back to her by the shoreline.

Abe sat down again, on the beach. Sand stuck to his sweaty palms. He was again, feeling slightly woozy. He swallowed and shook it off.

"What happened? Abe, Abe, darling, are you okay? Do you need me to call 911?"

He looked up. It was Alexis. She asked, "What on earth is going on? Why are you sitting down? You look a bit pale! Good Heavens, what's that thing, there in your hand?"

Abe felt folded paper in his left hand. Taking his readers out of his shirt pocket, he blinked to clear his eyes. He looked at a stiff, folded, legal sized parchment. With jittery fingers, he unfolded it and read the content. His mouth and throat went dry, more arid than the sand he sat upon. He could utter only a frog-like croak. Quick thinking Alexis reached into her bag and produced a thermos flask of ice water.

He gratefully took several swigs of cold water from the flask. He thanked her for always taking it with her on the beach, hooked onto her shoulder bag strap. He held the document out to her.

She read it. It was a deed to a two-acre warehouse, built on a five-acre lot, on Commercial Street. Her husband was listed as sole owner. Stapled to the document was a Collier County Tax Collector statement of estimated taxes. Scotch-taped, at the bottom, was a large, antique brass key, etched with his initials. "Great God Almighty," she gasped.

Abe began to laugh. He sat and laughed like a fool for fifteen seconds. Some walkers, nervously took a circular route about them. Out of breath, Abe stopped. He wiped his forehead with a kerchief. Then, he took the deed and key from her hand. She stared at him. She looked a little pale herself. She demanded, "Abe, just what the heck is going on? When and how did this thing get here, in your hand? Lord! Give me your hand and get up. Let's go home." She tightened her grip on his arm. They walked east to the condo.

"I'm going to call Doctor Bruce as soon as we get in. Are you sure you don't need a tablet of nitroglycerine?"

He stopped trudging along in the sand. He looked at her with love in his eyes. "No, I don't need nitro, sweetie, my heart is fine." He looked around then up to the sky, then turned to her again. "Honey, I am just so totally exhausted. But it's a good feeling However, I need a nap. That's all I want for now. When I wake up, I'll tell you all about it. Shit! It's so amazing. Even you probably won't believe a damned word. But, I'll tell you."

THE END

About the Author

Nick Kalvin

After a distinguished Medical career in Ohio and the Navy, where, as a Flight Surgeon, with VFP-62, he won the Presidential Unit Citation during the Cuban Missile Crisis, Nick Kalvin trained as an eye surgeon at Bascom Palmer Eye Institute. He became the 13th doctor at Naples Community Hospital in 1966 (when NCH was only a one-story structure and Naples had only one traffic light). He practiced in Naples for 34 years.

He has published articles about his medical research and poetry in collections. Motivated by current events, he wrote his recent debut novel, *SEXUAL JIHAD*, an adult adventure fiction about two tennis stars, kidnapped in Jihad to make sons for a Muslim Sheik, whose several wives produce only daughters. This timely book is now available at http://www.createspace.com/4875374 and Kindle/Amazon.

He is currently writing a sequel *CHAOS VS. THE CALIPHATE*. The first chapter of the sequel can be found at the end of *SEXUAL JIHAD*. He used research for *SEXUAL JIHAD* to write the short story, *CROSS CULTURE ROMANCE*. Are his works really fiction? Just look at current events today: beheadings, selling school girls as sex slaves, religious genocide, pre-teen brides, a new Caliphate rising like some Frankenstein from the past. Is the world falling back in time to 630 AD, the year Islamic expansion erupted?

Nick has been president of the Collier County Medical Society, NCH and the Florida Society of Ophthalmology. He is married to Judy Kalvin, has four sons, a daughter and eleven grandchildren. He plays tennis and cares for his fruit trees. He is still hungry to learn, at the age of eighty-three.

The Search for Hillman

Nancy Reges Murvine

The car looked like the dead carcass of an animal that had left its herd to find a peaceful place to die. Headlights like sunken eye sockets, the beast was slowly returning to the earth, decomposing tires slipping down into the scruffy tufts of autumn grasses. Even the sky, a silent witness to life's cycle, appeared to hold the moist last breaths of the dying in its bloated clouds. All of which justified Jason's flutter of nerves as he approached.

His Uncle Harry had told him stories about the car many times over the years. She was a foreigner, an English car Harry had shipped all the way to New York, where he had picked her up and driven cross country to surprise the woman he wanted to spend his life with. Apparently, she did not have the same view of their future and had left for Rapid City with a banker before Harry's return. Once he joked, "At least I still got the car; I hear she's run through four husbands and is looking for a newer model."

He had chosen the Hillman station wagon over the sedan to comfortably hold the family which he saw as including "at least three kids and two hunting dogs." Instead, Uncle Harry lived his life alone aside from the dozen or so stray dogs and one injured coyote who found their way down his dusty lane over the years since he abandoned the car and his dreams.

His story, or versions of it as the years passed, never carried regret or bitterness. "It's the way life goes," was the final word on nearly every chapter, including the one about how he had hitched his horse to the bumper and driven the car out to pasture because he needed the barn space it was taking up ten years after he bought it.

It was another ten years before Jason began his search, a seven-year-old who couldn't believe his Uncle Harry's promise of a car "that's all yours if you want it. And if you can find her." Like some mysterious, mythological creature, the Hillman had become worth her weight in gold if not in bragging rights. He surely did want her! And Jason had hunted for the treasure every summer he was sent to visit Uncle Harry on his massive Dakota ranch. Jason loved the freedom of hundreds of square miles for a city kid to explore. Unlike his fretful parents, his uncle encouraged him to "take a horse and run wild." "Be back in time for dinner" was a mere suggestion rather than a steadfast rule. By the time he was twelve, Jason was spending more of his vacations in the open ranges than at his uncle's house. With a good horse, well-provisioned for camping, Jason would rabidly be on the hunt for days at a time. Over the years, he marked off large sections of his uncle's land with X's on a handmade map to remind him of where he had been and where he would go next. But the car had always eluded him even as her legend grew in his mind.

Until he turned sixteen. That was the summer "Uncle Harry" was replaced simply with "Harry," one of many brazen ways to assert to the world "I am a man." That was the same summer he convicted Harry of being a liar. Harry had handed Jason a picture of the Hillman he had spotted in an auto traders' magazine. "That's her. Still a beauty." In that moment, the legend dissolved. The car was a square box with a grill as grotesque as the Cheshire Cat with braces. No style, homely even, certainly not a treasure. But rather than accept this true version of his childish obsession, Jason insisted there was no car. There had never been a car. He was old enough to know when he was being made a fool of and he didn't like it. He had better things to do with his time. He demanded that his uncle stop the game. Harry had shrugged and walked off the porch to the barn with a casual, "suit yourself; but she's out there and she's yours if you want her." Jason never went looking again.

Summer vacations with Harry shifted to vacations in more exotic locales with his college buddies and then his fiancé and now his family. He heard about Harry's death through his mother. She understood if he was too busy to attend the funeral, but she could use his help cleaning out her brother's homestead. Jason had flown out a week later. His son Theo begged to go along. Only six, he had never been west of the Mississippi. Aside from the high-rise canyon vistas of New York City where they lived, he had only seen coastal shorelines and the imaginary landscapes of Disney World.

It had been twenty years since Jason had last been on the property, but its magic returned through the eyes of his son. "Whoa, dad, this is awesome," rang with a reverence Jason remembered from the first time he set out on horseback. Today he and Theo were taking the Land Rover over stretches of land that reached cleanly to the horizon with no interruption other than an occasional volunteer tree or clump of brush. A few days ago, while he was cleaning out his uncle's den, Jason had found his old map, rolled neatly in a tube marked "Jason's Hunt for Hillman." It sat unfurled in his son's lap now as they bounced along old ruts made by horses or dry creek beds or maybe some unknown, divine plan.

"Tell me again what we're looking for, Dad?"

"A Hillman." Theo smiled at what he thought was a joke considering such flat land, but then his father slammed on the brakes and the press of the shoulder harness held Theo hard against the seat.

Jason took out the binoculars, adjusted the lens for distance, and then looked at his son. "Hang on, Theo." Ruts became springboards, bounces became leaps. Something had caught his father's attention. Theo's heart raced. He strained to follow his father's focus. Then he saw it. Something big, hunched in the field. A horse?

Jason did not drive right up to the car, leaving a respectful distance between the living and the dead. A tingling in his fingers made him fumble with the keys as he shut off the engine. The pulsing in Jason's ears muffled his son's voice. "Dad, you OK?"

He nodded and opened the door. Theo joined him, standing in front of the Land Rover. "It's the car, isn't it, Dad?" He raced ahead, small explosions of dust discharged with every stride. Jason's steps were more deliberate, heavy measures of his emotions. This was, indeed, the Hillman. Looking at its ancient, rusting body now, he did not see his teenaged, dismissive complaints of her plainness. He saw a sturdy, faithful rendition of his uncle's life.

Theo had jarred the passenger door open and was leaning in. "Dad, come here!" Jason stood beside him, following the path of his son's pointed finger to the open glove compartment. A small, blue velvet box, tied with a small bow held center stage. "It's like a treasure, Dad!" He reached in to take it.

"Leave it, son."

"Why? It might be gold or something."

Jason wanted to quote his uncle: "It's just the way it goes." But he could not explain that this box and this car and this land were all parts of his uncle's story and nothing should separate such things from each other. Instead, he smiled. "Yup, it could be gold. But why spoil the mystery." He took his son's hand and coaxed him back to the Land Rover. "Come on. It's getting late, and we promised your grandmother we would be home in time for dinner."

THE END

The Collector

Nancy Reges Murvine

Lucy was the perfect youngster. Nearly four, she was a bit small for her age but already very clever and precociously independent. And in a neighborhood where friendliness and trust could have been cross street names, it was not unusual to find Lucy in someone else's yard. When she was younger, someone would walk her home; now they were as likely to simply send her on her own way. When the neighborhood women gathered for tea and muffins on a weekend morning, Lucy would make a brief appearance in the kitchen, usually just long enough to enjoy one of Mrs. Wallis's homemade yogurt scones. Then Lucy would be off to the playroom where she easily kept herself entertained while the women went happily back to uninterrupted stories of their weeks. Sometimes Lucy would insert herself between the men as they sat screaming at football players on the big screen TV. Maybe it was their loud, baritone voices or her short attention span, but she would lose interest quickly, slide off the sofa, and return to her latest toy. Lucy loved her toys. And there were many. Far too many.

And that was the problem.

They called her the "collector." It was a kinder more endearing term than the accurate one. Lucy was a thief. Some might call her a kleptomaniac because she seemed truly unable to help herself; her willpower was nil when it came to leaving the property of others alone, and her heists

126

were often carried out right under the noses of unsuspecting friends and neighbors.

At times, she was a hero of sorts. She had found Mrs. Johnston's wedding band after she lost it tending the leafy lettuces in her garden. Once Mr. Harrington had taken off his watch to join his kids in their above ground pool. He eventually gave up looking for it in the tall weeds that surrounded the base of the bright blue pool frame. Lucy had already taken it home for safekeeping. There were eyeglass cases, a lost wallet, and tickets to a concert, all dropped from pockets or purses and later reunited with grateful owners.

Once she had come home with a cheap, white milk glass vase taken from Mrs. Pryor's front porch. The freshly cut tulips that had been in it could not be found. The miracle was that the vase made it into Lucy's pillaged pile without a scratch. She had cradled it a full block without dropping it, assurance of the value she placed on every find. That night, Lucy had a little diarrhea with the requisite lesson on diets which should not include flowers. She listened with earnest intent, but, in truth, she did not follow the conversation or understand the lecture.

Of course, Lucy was always reprimanded—manners and standards of decency were expected in this family—and she hung her head in guilt and shame as was required. And there were consequences. Lucy would be made to take every item she collected out to the front porch and set it on the steps. Little items were gathered in a basket. Others, like the wooden doll that Mr. Williams swore Lucy had to have come into their house to take, perched on separate treads so they could easily be identified and retrieved by their rightful owners. If anything was missing in the neighborhood, everyone knew where to look first. Sometimes, Lucy would be sitting on the steps when someone came up to claim their missing object. Because she looked adorable, not criminal, the owners, more often than not, would smile and tousle her little blonde head before heading off down the block. The double message of shame and appreciation made giving up her crooked ways that much harder.

Then events took a drastic turn.

Lucy especially liked collecting things that made noise. If a ball squeaked, she would hide it for as long as she could. A wind chime; it was hers. Even the McLean's heavy dinner bell nearly made it back to Lucy's house until her little legs grew tired of hauling the clanging brute. But it was little Davy Blake's rattle that caused all the trouble. Davy's mom saw Lucy at the end of her walkway. "Hey there, Lucy," was all the invitation she needed to hang around. Maybe they'd even invite her to go to the park with them. Lucy loved the park. As Davy's mom turned for a second to pull a ringing cell phone from her pocket, Lucy eyed the rattle that kept disappearing under Davy's light blanket with its rocket ships. There was no telling what Lucy was thinking, but fast as lightning she whipped the blanket away, with Davy unfortunately tangled in the last of the swaddling. Out of the stroller he tumbled. Lucy took off for home, with the wailing Davy and distraught mom fading into the background.

But Lucy's roaming, thieving days were over. This attempted robbery had nearly cracked open an innocent child's skull. Authorities were called. It was implied that Lucy's lack of supervision verged on neglect and one of the officers strongly suggested that a fence be installed so Lucy could be watched. What next, one of those silly leashes tethered to an adult every time she left the yard?

Oh, did I forget to mention that Lucy is a golden retriever?

THE END

128

About the Author

Nancy Reges Murine

Like so many who have made their homes in paradise, I am a transplant. I lived in Delaware where I taught middle school English and writing for many years. The state of Delaware Arts Council awarded me a grant as an emerging artist, and so I have emerged as a published writer of poetry, short stories, and educational essays. In my new home state of Florida, I recently won a short story award from *Florida Weekly*. Currently, I am multitasking on a volume of short stories as well as a second novel in a three-part series.

I can be reached for workshops or readings via e-mail at: authormurvine@embarqmail.com

IS THAT YOU, MISS C?

Virginia Colwell Read

It was warm for this early in the year. She kicked her covers off and rolled over onto her back. The sheer curtains puffed lazily in and out from the slight breeze coming in through the open window of her apartment. She enjoyed the breeze fingering her naked body, but it did little to cool it. She should get up, but it was pleasant to lie here listening to the birds' chatter in the Dogwood tree outside the window.

She decided to celebrate this spring morning by wearing her pretty, pink and white flowered dress with the frilly collar and ruffles down the front. The pink pumps and the big, pink bow for her hair would be the perfect accessories. Flowery, frilly, billowing dresses and bows were not what a two hundred twenty-two-pound woman should be wearing, but long ago she had decided to wear what she loved and let the rest of the world think what they wanted to think.

Sliding her legs over the side of the bed, she sat up. Without reaching for her robe, she stood and padded through the living room to the door of her apartment. Before dressing, she always retrieved the *New York Times* outside her door and carried it back to the kitchen to work its crossword puzzle while eating breakfast.

Opening the door part way, she bent down and reached for the paper. No paper. She stretched her arm out as far as she could and waggled it back and forth across the floor. No paper.

That paper boy! She wanted to throttle him. Time after time, she'd asked him to leave her paper right at her door and not throw it from the stairway. Opening the door wider, she poked her head out to see on which side of the door it had landed. No paper. She moved further into the hall and saw her paper lying on the floor almost at the next apartment. This was really too much. She would complain to the paper this time.

The hall was empty. It was still early. No one on her floor was up yet. Looking both ways, she stepped out and dashed down the hall. Just as she bent over to pick up the paper, she heard a door slam. Panicked, she grabbed the paper and ran back to her apartment. The door was closed.

She grabbed for the knob and twisted. Too late, she remembered she had not switched the lock on the door to unlock. She leaned against the door and tried to think. What to do? Her mind raced over her options.

The sleazy-eyed janitor had a key, but he was four flights down. No way was she going to walk naked down four flights of stairs and knock on his door. Meeting him in the hall was her limit. He would look pop-eyed down her bosom and try to find an excuse to rub up against her and he was always finding excuses to get in her apartment. The janitor was out.

Jeff, in the next apartment, worked a late shift and usually slept with ear plugs and eye shades until mid-afternoon. It was doubtful that pounding on his door and shouting would rouse him, but it would certainly rouse the rest of the floor.

The apartment across the hall belonged to the snooty Van Duzens. They found it difficult to even say "Good Day." The last time they met in the hall, Mrs. Van Duzen pointedly said, "You should use less rouge on your cheeks and wear more appropriate dresses. You look like a whore. People will think this is a brothel." What would she think now?

The apartment next to them belonged to Tom, a newly divorced man. Shortly after he'd moved in, he'd knocked on her door with drinks in hand. "Just want to be friendly," he

131

said. Once inside, he became friendly all right. She definitely wasn't going to ask him for help.

The retired professor in the end apartment was her only hope. He wore a black patch over one eye. Supposedly, his vision was impaired. Hopefully, his sexuality too, but that was somewhat dubious. He left early every morning to eat breakfast and read his paper at the drug store on the corner. She suspected that the young girls going to school and the young women on their way to work were the real attraction. Nevertheless, he was her best choice. There was nothing to do now but wait until he made an appearance.

While she waited, she tried to fashion some sort of covering from the pages of *The Times.* She wrapped several sections around her, trying to position them to cover her ample flesh. The pages either kept slipping down or tore. Torn, crinkled paper covered her feet, and with only two hands it was impossible to cover her boobs and lower parts at the same time.

She decided that when she heard someone in the hall, she would turn and face the wall. That way she wouldn't have to look at any one and they would only see her back. She hoped she wouldn't have to stand here much longer. Goosebumps covered her body, but did little to hide anything. Hearing the noise of a door opening and closing, she quickly turned and faced the wall. With closed eyes, she listened as the steps came closer and then stopped.

"Is that you, Miss C?"

"Yes, it's me."

"Well, good morning to you. I'm on my way to the drug store for my paper and breakfast. Have a nice day."

"Professor, I need you to do something for me."

"I'll be happy to do what I can to help a lady. Leave a note for me in my mail box."

"NO! Don't go. I need you to help me right now."

"Are you in trouble, Miss C?"

"Yes. I'm locked out of my apartment."

"Well, I'm sorry to hear that, Miss C."

"I need a key to unlock my door."

"I'm sorry Miss C but I don't know anything about locks. If your apartment's locked, you better talk to the janitor."

"That's what I want you to do. I want you to ask the janitor for the key to my apartment."

"It's nice of you to offer to give me your key, but I think it's better if we keep our own keys."

"I don't want your key. I just want the janitor's key to my apartment."

"I don't know why you need two keys, but I'll be happy to tell the janitor you want another key."

"I don't want another key. I need you to ask the janitor for HIS KEY to my apartment and have him give HIS KEY to YOU. Then YOU bring the key up to me."

"I'll be happy to do that. "Always ready to help a damsel in distress." I'll stop on my way back from my morning errands and pick it up."

"Professor, I need that key right now. NOW! Not tomorrow."

"Well, things are usually better by tomorrow."

The sound of his squeaky shoes echoed in the empty hall. She turned in time to see his head disappear as he made his way down the stairs.

THE END

About the Author

Virginia Colwell Read

Virginia Colwell Read was born in Auburn in the Finger Lakes District of New York state. She taught school in Arlington, Virginia after graduating from Mary Washington College of University of Virginia. She then worked for the government where one of her jobs was writing the daily synopsis of activities behind the Iron Curtin for the President of the US, the Vice President, the Joint Chiefs of Staff, and the Directors of NSA and CIA. In the sixties, she moved with her husband to Milwaukee, Wisconsin where she raised their four children and an assortment of animals.

During her years of volunteer work she edited many organizational newsletters and reports of her work on archaeological sites. She has written an article for the *Milwaukee Historical Messenger*, three short stories and two poems for *Creative Wisconsin: A Literary Magazine*; a story and two poems in *Stories to Read to Your Grandchildren*; and received two first places for children, a second place, and an Honorable Mention for poetry in the Florida AAUW creative writing contests. She moved to Marco Island permanently in 1982 and is interested in photography, gardening, archaeology, historical preservation and material culture.

My Safari—An Animal Lover's Tribute

Ellen Redd

On my safari, I did not journey to a distant land, but stayed right here in the United States. Actually, my safari is an ongoing adventure, where I visit zoos, animal sanctuaries, cat shelters, farms, and even homes to appreciate the animals that enrich our world.

I am fortunate to live on a beautiful island surrounded by flowers and palm trees, between blue skies and blue waters. As a bonus, Marco Island is also a habitat for many of Florida's wonderful animals—cute little burrowing owls, adventurous sea turtles, majestic bald eagles, industrious gopher tortoises, adaptable spotted bobcats, elusive panthers.

With family and friends, I take advantage of my home's beauty. We frequently visit the Naples Zoo, the Conservancy of Southwest Florida, Rookery Bay, and many other places in Naples and Marco Island. We appreciate the sea turtle protection work and keep up on the news from the Conservancy where injured birds are brought to heal before being returned to the wild. We are heartened when we hear about rescues of turtles, eagles, dolphins, and other animals.

For thousands of years, we humans have appreciated the animals that share our world. Cave paintings from more than 30,000 years ago provide many examples of animals that were beloved or respected by ancient peoples in the same manner that we treat our pets today.

I've watched and admired animals in many habitats—in my home, on farms, at shelters, in sanctuaries and zoos. I grew up on a farm in a family of animal lovers. Whenever a homeless dog or cat wandered onto our farm, we offered food, a warm bed, and a home. Our pets were so numerous that I can't even remember all of their names, but each was much loved.

We also had many farm animals. As children, we were taught to care for orphaned animals or those with special needs. When I was 10 years old, I helped raise an orphaned calf. My sister, brother, and I took turns rising at 5 a.m. to feed the baby calf before heading to school. We dubbed the calf 'Queen Mary' and she grew strong and healthy. We also raised a baby pig, rejected by his mother because of a deformed foot. Along with our dogs, Sir Walter, the pig, limping slightly, followed us all around the farm.

Noel, our horse, arrived on Christmas Day. She was large and gentle, the perfect horse for children. We enjoyed many leisurely horseback rides on summer days. One of my father's friends raised thoroughbreds. Occasionally, he would come to our farm towing a trailer with a spirited thoroughbred onboard. We would fly through the sunny, green fields with the thoroughbred's mane and tail flowing.

When I first read Dylan Thomas' "Fern Hill" about "the spellbound horses walking warm out of the whinnying green stable on to the fields of praise," I thought he must have been writing about the farm of my childhood because that's how I pictured it then, and still do.

We were taught the importance of treating farm animals humanely. These animals sustain human life in so many ways, and we tried to support only those businesses that provided animals with a clean and healthy environment. To this day, I check whether companies use suppliers that follow guidelines requiring animals be raised in safety and comfort. Companies should articulate to their suppliers that animal abuse is intolerable. Suppliers should guarantee that animals are given abundant fresh water, a healthy diet, and live in an environment with sufficient space for stress-free living.

While I was farm-grown, my husband grew up in a city. Farm animals were not part of his youth, but cats were family. Cats who appeared meowing at their door were welcomed inside for food, shelter, and a good home.

Over the years, we have volunteered at several cat shelters and adopted cats from those shelters. We have done the everyday jobs of maintaining the shelters and caring for the cats, as well as raising funds for various events to support shelters.

In addition to advocating responsible standards for raising farm animals and providing good homes for pets, we've been long-time supporters of zoos around the country and world. We've visited zoos in Munich, Washington DC, Bronx, Cincinnati, San Diego, Indianapolis, Naples, Florida, and many other places. We've joined zoos in Cincinnati, Indianapolis, and Washington DC as members.

Some critics of zoos argue that zoo animals should live in the wild in their natural environments where they can roam freely. Unfortunately, these habitats continue to shrink thanks to human encroachment. The areas animals have for hunting food is decreasing in size. Animals that were once plentiful are now endangered because they struggle to survive in territories too small to support them.

For one example, per the Defenders of Wildlife web site (defenders.org), in 1900, the number of cheetahs in the world was about 100,000. Today, their number has declined to an estimated 9,000 to 12,000 cheetahs in the wild. These beautiful creatures, the fastest land mammals in the world, are vulnerable to becoming an endangered species as their habitats continue to shrink.

Humans often develop strong emotional ties with zoo animals, especially baby animals. No matter how fierce a large adult animal can be, baby animals are endearing. A baby animal that is sick or born premature or otherwise needs human help grips our hearts. With hope and apprehension, we watch their struggles as their lives unfold, and we champion them as they grow strong.

Social media invites us to participate in many events that we probably would not even know about otherwise. Along with more than a million other viewers, we awaited the birth of a baby for April, a giraffe at the Animal Adventure Park in upstate New York. People commented that they woke up in the middle of the night to check whether April's baby had been born. When Bao Bao, the panda born at the Smithsonian's National Zoo, left for China, social media let us bid her farewell. Views from eagle cams enable us to look inside bald eagles' nests and watch the eggs hatch and the babies grow into fledglings.

As members of the Cincinnati Zoo, we have seen many stories about baby animals that have survived thanks to Zoo caregivers. Take the story of little Fiona, a hippopotamus born six weeks premature at the Cincinnati Zoo. Fiona's weight was dangerously low at birth; she didn't have the strength to swim or walk. Thankfully, she was born on land instead of in the water, which is the normal environment for hippo births, so keepers were able to take baby Fiona to a special nursery where they could give her 24-hour care.

Caregivers were deeply attached to their baby and provided a daily blog to communicate with Fiona's followers. Each day, the blog brought news of Fiona's progress and setbacks. As time passed, the number of Fiona's supporters grew. At one point, caregivers felt that Fiona had survived enough milestones that they could decrease the frequency of blog updates. When the blog writer announced that the daily updates would cease, the outcry was so intense that the writers did an immediate U-turn and agreed to continue the daily blog. The daily news release became known as the 'Fiona Fix' because followers were addicted to their daily updates about the adorable hippo. Fiona was a phenomenon.

Fiona required skilled veterinary care. Veterinarians checked Fiona when she became lethargic or when her appetite was not good. When it was determined that Fiona was not getting enough oxygen, veterinarians prescribed supplemental oxygen. Fiona's daily blog showed one of her devoted caregivers even teaching breathing lessons by letting Fiona lie on top of her to better understand how to breathe. Caregivers helped Fiona learn to float in the water by supervising her in pools of water. Experts at Cincinnati Children's Hospital placed IVs into Fiona's tiny veins when she became dehydrated. In addition to regular bottle feedings for Fiona, zoo staff regularly rubbed lotion on Fiona to hydrate her skin.

As news about Fiona spread via social media and television, she became a worldwide celebrity. Facebook and Twitter fans expressed love and devotion for the baby and deep gratitude to Fiona's caregivers. Followers sent prayers and well wishes for Fiona. Supporters cheered when Fiona took her first steps, her first swim, cut her first teeth, napped on her caregivers. On Valentine's Day, Fiona received many greetings on social media and from Cincinnati school children. The principal tuba player at the Cincinnati Symphony Orchestra played Brahms' Lullaby for Fiona. Every sound the growing hippo made was greeted enthusiastically. People bought Fiona shirts, Fiona magnets, Fiona cookies, Fiona playing cards, Fiona stuffed animals, and many other keepsakes. Fiona cocktail recipes were created. Fans wrote letters to their favorite celebrity, Fiona, and keepers published photos of reading these letters to Fiona.

Fiona's story is not the only story about animal celebrities at the Cincinnati Zoo. When three rare Malayan tiger cubs were born at the Zoo in February 2017, keepers found that the first-time mother had no idea how to care for her cubs. When the mother neglected her tiny newborns, keepers took the babies to the nursery.

When a keeper noticed that one of these tiger cubs could not hold up her head without difficulty, a chiropractor was called to align the little cub's neck. The young cub was named Chira, in honor of her chiropractor, and she is now developing and roughhousing with her siblings. These beautiful cats are critically endangered, with fewer than 500 remaining in the world. Zoo visitors can watch these tigers play and run and grow in a friendly environment instead of leaving them to an uncertain future in a vanishing habitat.

One of my favorite success stories from the Cincinnati Zoo involves a baby cheetah named Redd. Redd was one of five premature cheetah cubs born in March 2016. Tragically, the cubs' mother, Willow, did not survive childbirth, and two of the babies lived only a short time. For Redd, the smallest of the surviving cubs, the early days were touch-and-go. In order to get proper nourishment, Redd had a feeding tube, and he was easily identified because he wore a shirt to protect his feeding tube. In his fashionable attire, little Redd quickly became a very popular cheetah. His health challenges and his extraordinary beauty quickly brought him celebrity status. When Redd was finally strong enough to eat on his own without the feeding tube, fans from far and wide celebrated Redd's graduation to the next step.

After months in the nursery, Redd and his sisters, Kathryn and Willow, moved from the nursery to the cheetah yard. The move was photographed and followed intensely by Redd's fans. In the cheetah yard, the triplets entered the Cat Ambassador Program along with several other cheetahs. As cat ambassadors, the cheetahs develop their running skills in the cheetah yards. They also learn to ride in vans so that they can visit schools and educate children.

Unfortunately, however, Redd was in for more challenges in his young life. After he moved to the cheetah yard, veterinarians discovered that Redd had an abnormal hip bone. He underwent surgery to remove the abnormal bone. When a photo appeared showing the little cub's shaved hip, which is spotted like his magnificent fur, Redd's followers were frantic with worry about their beautiful little cheetah. After therapy and daily exercises, however, Redd's energy and mobility returned. He now plays with his siblings, Kathryn and Willow, and his friend, Donni, in the cheetah yards. While Redd may not be the fastest cheetah, he can run and enjoy life as a normal cheetah. Because of his successes in overcoming struggles, Redd is an inspiration and an excellent ambassador for his species. Redd will always have a piece of my heart and the hearts of thousands of followers.

The Cincinnati Zoo is one of several zoos in the United States that provides homes for cheetahs. Cheetahs in captivity live longer than in the wild where the cubs are prey for larger animals and targets for poachers. Also, in the zoo, cheetahs are not forced to hunt. Instead, they can savor their meals without guarding their hard-won dinner from other animals.

Good zoos cherish these beautiful animals, providing an environment as close to their original habitats as possible, and they give them space to run and be normal cheetahs. The Cincinnati Zoo has a farm that enables the cheetahs to breed and develop surrounded by wooded acres away from people. Many cheetahs prefer solitude, and the farm provides the desired solitude. Zoo caregivers visit the farm to make certain that the cheetahs are well and have food; otherwise, they give these cheetahs privacy to enjoy life in the wild without the hardships they encounter in their natural habitats.

The Cincinnati Zoo has also established the Angel Fund to support cheetahs in their natural habitats. This fund was named in honor of Angel, the first cheetah in the Cat Ambassador Program (CAP). Cat Ambassadors visit schools and other organizations to educate people about cheetahs. In 2012, Savanna, a cheetah at the Cincinnati Zoo, even appeared on the Today Show to introduce cheetahs.

The Cincinnati Zoo is one of several zoos that pair dogs with baby cheetahs. Blakely, an Australian Shepherd at the Cincinnati Zoo, stepped up to be a friend and playmate for the three orphaned cheetahs, Redd, Kathryn, and Willow. When Donni, a cheetah from Oregon, came to the Cincinnati Zoo because his mother abandoned him, Donni was paired with a chocolate Labrador named Moose. Donni and Moose became fast friends, playing and chasing each other. In

February, Donni and Moose celebrated their birthdays with a birthday cake for each made with their favorite ingredients.

After Redd, Kathryn, and Willow left the nursery, Blakely remained to help with other babies who needed him. Dale, a [1]baby takin, learned socialization skills from Blakely. Wallabies, an ocelot, a warthog, skunks, and the three rare Malayan tiger cubs, mentioned previously, also benefited from Blakely's care, in addition to other baby animals.

First, Blakely had to teach the three energetic, young tigers to play nicely to prevent their sharp claws and teeth from hurting him. When Chira, Batari, and Izzy, the three cubs, grew strong enough to leave the nursery, they had learned behaviors from Blakely that their tiger mother would have taught them.

Obviously, the climates for the Cincinnati Zoo in Ohio and the Naples Zoo in Florida are quite different. The Naples Zoo showcases animals that live comfortably in the Southwest Florida climate. Florida with its year-round warmth is teeming with an abundance of animals from dangerous alligators to invasive pythons to magnificent panthers to majestic bald eagles. The sheer variety of the birds, mammals, and reptiles is staggering, and the Naples Zoo provides a wonderful setting for people to see these animals.

One of my favorite residents at the Naples Zoo is Uno, a rare Florida panther. When only two-years old, Uno was blinded by a shotgun blast. He was found wandering along a busy road, emaciated and weak. Uno has moved to the Naples Zoo permanently, where he is an animal ambassador. Uno reminds us of the importance of helping these beautiful animals and working to conserve their natural habitats.

The Naples Zoo is the closest zoo for Marco Island locals, but we can watch over many animals that share our island. Each spring, we look for eaglets at the Marco Eagle Sanctuary. When we spot the adult eagles, Paleo and Calusa,

---

[1] A goat-antelope found in the eastern Himalayas.

142

at their nest feeding an eaglet, we begin watching daily for signs of development. A fledging's first flight is both very exciting and very stressful. When an eaglet takes test flights, we watch anxiously and hope intensely for the young bird's safety until the fledgling has mastered the skills of flying and fishing in the nearby bays.

Marco Island is home for gopher tortoises and burrowing owls, and Marco Island residents protect these fine creatures. Gopher tortoises are good citizens because they dig burrows that other Florida species, such as the adorable burrowing owls, can use. With their strong, shovel-like front legs, these tortoises create burrows that are large and deep. Gopher tortoises are also civic-minded in pruning the plants they eat so that the plants grow new, healthy foliage.

Our sea waters are enriched by the sea turtles that lay their eggs on Florida's beaches. Sea turtles eat the sea grass, encouraging growth and maintaining its health. Sea turtles are some of our most adventurous animals, traveling thousands of miles in the vast oceans. We, in Marco Island, protect the sea turtles by fencing their nests on the beaches. Homeowners living on the beach dim lights at night during nesting season so that the sea turtles do not become disoriented and wander towards the artificial lights rather than the horizon.

Two large cats native to Florida are the Florida panther and the bobcat. The bobcat is smaller than the panther and can be identified by a bobbed tail and fringe of fur around the head. While the bobcat is abundant in North America, the Florida panther is critically endangered. Destruction of their habitats by humans and traffic accidents have endangered these beautiful cats.

A piece of encouraging news, though, is that Florida panthers are expanding their territories. In March 2017, the news reported sighting a female panther with two cubs north of the Caloosahatchee River. Estimates for the number of panthers in southern Florida range between only 100 and 200.

Florida has an amazing abundance of very beautiful birds, from songbirds, wading birds, waterfowl, and seabirds, to raptors and owls. I'll never forget the sunset cruise with Rookery Bay and seeing the Rookery Island where hundreds of birds fly in at dusk. It amazed me to see islands devoid of birds all around the Rookery Island; yet, I couldn't spot a tree branch at the Rookery Island without chattering birds.

Florida's warm waters are favorable for manatees, but manatees often travel long distances into cold waters. Take the example of the adventurous manatee that showed up in the Chesapeake Bay. Called Chessie, he was rescued, and returned to Florida when weather began to turn cold. Then, when warmer weather came, Chessie traveled north again, but, this time, he returned to Florida on his own when he got cold.

The Cincinnati Zoo is one of several zoos that work with the US Fish and Wildlife Service to rehabilitate sick and injured manatees. Abigail came to the Cincinnati Zoo suffering from cold. After rehabilitation at the Cincinnati Zoo, Abigail was able to return to Florida. These delightful mammals are very slow, and often casualties of boats. Florida boaters are asked to obey speed limits to avoid hurting or killing manatees.

Giant pandas can be found in a few zoos in this country. We have traveled many miles to visit these vulnerable animals, which are dependent on continued conservation efforts. Our journeys have not yet extended to China where giant pandas are native. China protects their treasured pandas by creating refuge areas that offer safe environments where the pandas live and breed. Logging is banned in these reserves to protect bamboo, which is the pandas' primary food. Within the reserves are large areas so that when bamboo in one area dies, the pandas can migrate to other areas within the reserve. People patrol the reserves to provide medical care, if needed; they also research panda behavior and educate people about these adorable animals.

China has given or leased giant pandas to many zoos throughout the world. When China gives or loans a giant panda to a zoo in another country, the agreement often states that any offspring must move to China at a certain age. Thus was the case with little Bao Bao, who had to go to China prior to turning 4 years old. The Smithsonian's National Zoo hosted a huge farewell celebration in honor of Bao Bao before she left for China in February 2017.

Many zoos have Panda cams so that people can take peeks at these cuddly, bear-like animals. Be sure to check out a Panda cam on a day when you need a smile.

Along with other organizations, zoos support threatened or endangered species throughout the world. For example, the Cincinnati Zoo works with Panthera, an organization devoted to conserving wild cats and their environments. In Malaysia, Panthera is training rangers to install camera traps in forests to help capture poachers. In Colombia, Panthera is working with ranchers to breed cattle to defend themselves against jaguars. This project is challenging, but it is showing promise of success. If the jaguars cannot kill the cattle, the farmers have no reason to kill the jaguars.

Many zoos in this country are working to protect natural habitats of animals. Zoos provide funds for conservation projects all over the world and also send staff members to work in the field. Zoos in this country work on projects in the Congo, Malaysia, New Zealand, Guatemala, Madagascar, and many other countries to help save endangered species.

Since animals rely on conservation measures, conservation is a crucial goal for many zoos. Major initiatives within zoos include using solar power, reducing water usage, recycling, changing to LED lights, using pervious pavements, promoting sustainable palm oil, incorporating sustainable building materials, and more.

The Cincinnati Zoo has many conservation efforts. For example, more than 6,000 solar panels form the roof over the Zoo's parking lot, and these solar panels provide about 25% of the Zoo's energy.

The Environmental Protection Agency uses the Cincinnati Zoo's storm water management system as a model for other organizations. The Zoo's efforts in reducing their water usage has resulted in saving one billion gallons of water over the past decade. Storm water systems are buried underneath the Painted Dog Valley, where a 400,000-gallon rain tank provides 25% of the Zoo's water. Pavers are made of pervious materials so that storm water seeps through the surface. Rainwater sitting below the Zoo is used for garden irrigation, pools for the animals, moats, and waterfalls.

We may not realize how many foods from bread to ice cream use palm oil, the world's most popular vegetable oil. Palm oil is in soaps, cosmetics, bio-fuels, and many other items. Palm oil trees grow in Indonesia and Malaysia, which are native habitats for tigers, elephants, rhinos, orangutans, and a wide diversity of other animals. Habitats are being destroyed to extract the oil, which threatens the animals with extinction.

Palm oil can be produced in a sustainable manner in order to preserve the forests and water. Zoos are educating people about the importance of using sustainable palm oil in order to preserve the environment for the wildlife. The Roundtable on Sustainable Palm Oil (RSPO) certifies sustainable palm oil, and companies use labels that show whether the palm oil in their products has been certified. Consumers can check RSPO.ORG for information about compliance with RSPO's requirements.

Zoos remind us of the importance of a clean environment and a sustainable lifestyle. Zoos are leading the way with policies that promote water conservation, solar energy, recycling, sustainable food sources, and many other initiatives.

When I watch the challenges of innocent baby animals that depend on humans for life, I cheer them on. As they struggle, I applaud their efforts and those of their caregivers. I have been inspired by the stories of Redd, the cheetah, and his sisters, Willow and Kathryn, Fiona, the hippopotamus, the Malayan tiger cubs, Chira, Batari, and Izzy, the takin, Dale, and many other baby animals. These little animals require the expert veterinary care and 24-hour attention that a good zoo can provide. For endangered animals that are threatened in their native habitats, a zoo is a safe haven.

Each spring, I watch the fledgling eagles in the Marco Eagle Sanctuary as they learn to fly and navigate their environment. Those initial flights are stressful, and I am thankful for people who watch over these majestic birds and help to rescue them when necessary. When I visit Uno, the Florida panther, I am grateful to the Naples Zoo for providing him with a sanctuary. I applaud the wonderful work of the Conservancy in rescuing and restoring injured Florida wildlife.

I'm very privileged to watch many animals in many habitats from households and farms to zoos. My travels do not take me to remote lands very often, but I can always admire and appreciate animals in my surroundings, as if on an exotic safari.

Each creature has a special purpose and a unique beauty. Many species are endangered, and the loss of one species impacts the whole in ways that we don't fully understand. We must protect natural habitats for the animals in our world. For zoo animals, we must provide sanctuaries with large outdoor areas so that animals can run, play, and enjoy the sunshine, while living in a safe and comfortable environment. My mission is to help safeguard the many wonderful creatures in our world.

THE END

The Era of the Publishing Lion

Ellen and Fleur-de-Lys Redd

1. Introduction to Rogersville

As we crossed Clinch Mountain on the way to Rogersville, Tennessee, we felt the customary awe that we experience at the beauty of the craggy mountain vista. As usual, we stopped at the top of the mountain to view the panorama of the distant lakes.

Fleur-de-Lys, our beautiful cat, had been a very pleasant traveling companion—sitting between us for the long drive with only an occasional meow demanding her favorite treats. Our car was geared for Fleur-de-Lys' comfort. The backseats fold flat so that her carrier and litter box fit perfectly and remain stable during travel. We provide food, water, toys, and, of course, treats, while she travels.

Fleur-de-Lys has thick blue-grey fur, gold eyes, and four, large polydactyl paws with thumbs on the two front paws. Her paws are handy with many sports. Racing and climbing are special talents, and some days, she likes to play the piano.

My sister's home is on a Rogersville farm, which was my childhood home, and she has cared for it wonderfully. My parents would be so proud if they could see their old home. When we visit, she and her family welcome us hospitably with delicious food and good conversation. We get up-to-speed as we talk about the activities in each of our lives.

Fleur-de-Lys' accommodation has a window with pleasant views, from where she can look at a pastoral scene of tall trees, colorful flowers, blooming shrubs, and farm animals. The cattle in a nearby field captivate her with their unusual sounds.

While in town, we fill our days visiting family and reacquainting ourselves with favorite places. As the second oldest town in the state of Tennessee, Rogersville is filled with history. The recently renovated Hale Springs Inn on Main Street in the middle of downtown has hosted presidents—Andrew Jackson, James K. Polk, and Andrew Johnson. This inn was built in 1824 and has been restored with great attention to detail. One day, we enjoyed a delicious meal at Amis Mill Eatery and went to the museum next door to see the Civil War artifacts assembled there. On other days, we joined friends for treats at Miss Bea's and Sweet Creams.

We walked along the paths of a lovely park called Crockett Spring Park and Arboretum. In the park is Rogers Cemetery where Joseph Rogers, founder of Rogersville, is buried with his wife, Mary Amis Rogers. The land was originally owned by David and Elizabeth Hedge Crockett, grandparents of David Crockett, the soldier and politician who died at the Alamo in 1836.

Rogersville was founded in 1775 before Tennessee was in the Union. At that time, Tennessee was in North Carolina. Then, from 1786 to 1788, Tennessee was in the State of Franklin before becoming part of Tennessee when Tennessee joined the Union in 1796.

After a visit to town, we were looking forward to seeing what Fleur-de-Lys had been doing. While we are away, Fleur-de-Lys stays busy. We have evidence of this because she leaves one of her toy mice on the area she wants us to notice. At any given time, she works on several research projects. Using meowcestry.cat, she has tracked her ancestors all over the globe and throughout many eras. She has mapped out her involved family tree and often writes about the experiences of her family members throughout history.

As we walked into Fleur-de-Lys' room, we saw that she had been doing research and writing. She had placed Noel mouse on top of the computer because she wanted us to read her work.

2. Fleur-de-Lys Presents

My aunt's home has a window that looks out on a very bucolic scene. Positioned in front of this window, I'm enjoying the peace and quiet. Then, my mother and father return to tell me about their adventures. They fully understand their status as staff animals, but I often refer to them as my mother and father, and will do so, at times, in this story.

We drive through Rogersville twice a year on the way from Kentucky to Florida and back again. Even though we are not in Rogersville during the Christmas season, my mother goes around humming "I'll Be Home for Christmas" and playing it on the piano. When she sings "I'll Be Home for Christmas," she is in Rogersville *if only in her dreams* as the words of the song say.

While my staff was out traipsing down memory lane, I was finding my own family memories in meowcestry.cat. As it turns out, my mother's ancestors who lived in Rogersville during the 1800s had roots in the Netherlands where one of my most adventurous ancestors was also born.

When Peter Stuyvesant arrived in New Amsterdam, now New York, in 1645, he brought several Dutch sailors with him. He also brought some very hardy, talented cats, and one of these energetic mousketeers was my long-ago ancestor, Bram. Bram was polydactyl, like myself. Polydactyl cats were especially useful on ships because that extra digit helped them do all of the ship's chores more quickly than other cats could do.

Food protection was one of Bram's main responsibilities, and he excelled at this task. The food supply was safe from all sneaky critters under Bram's zealous guard.

Bram was also a particularly gifted weather forecaster. He could sniff a storm coming hours before it happened so that the sailors could modify their course to avoid bad weather. Some of the sailors were wary of Bram's abilities and called him a magic spirit, but he accepted their comments with appreciation. This trait of weather prediction is common in many of my relatives. I, myself, was born with an uncanny ability to recognize a coming storm. When bad weather threatens, I sense it immediately. My mother sees my antsy behavior, and announces the weather report to my father. She calls me her personal barometer. I just smile and let her scratch my chin.

Because of his extraordinary leadership skills, Bram was promoted to Ship's Cat and designated the 'Captain's Assistant'. Even though he was an executive, Bram became very close friends with several of the sailors, offering a sense of camaraderie among them, which made everyone feel at home on the ship. This was no small accomplishment given the length of time for voyages across the ocean in those days.

Bram kept everything shipshape on that voyage. In accordance with his stature, Bram enjoyed excellent dining on the ship. He liked the rolled oats, but his favorite was herring, and he got lots of herring on the trip.

My reading about Bram was fascinating, and I realized that I inherited Bram's talents for organization. It is my responsibility to watch for birds landing on our balcony, and I am very accomplished in this task. I also help with entertaining guests by sitting in a chair and staring at any people that come around. I am an accomplished decorator and place bits of grey cat fur around the home. I also leave my toy mice in strategic places to make it easy for my people to know what I want them to notice.

But back to Bram—after he landed in New Amsterdam, Bram decided that he wanted to explore this new country. He had an adventurous streak. He headed south, staying close to the shoreline because he liked seafood and stopped in Maryland where he met a beautiful calico named Duchess. Bram and Duchess lived a long and happy life together and were blessed with a large family.

One of Bram's progeny established residence with a Dutch family in Maryland, and this family was a long-ago relative of my mother's family. This was a very fitting family for Bram's ancestors because the members of this family were, like Bram, very adventurous. In fact, the family uprooted their home in Maryland and took off for the promise of inexpensive land in Tennessee and Kentucky. The brave trailblazer, Daniel Boone, had earlier forged a path through the mountains of Kentucky, and the family followed this trail.

These adventurers traveled in a Conestoga wagon along with several other fortune seekers. Their journey was very difficult, especially in the mountainous regions. Just thinking about several horses pulling a wagon filled with supplies up and down steep hills is not an appealing thought. Going up a hill might be kind of like kneading, I guess— moving back and forth, back and forth until the wagon finally makes it over the hill. The downhill trip would be another story.

Bram's descendants settled with the adventurers in East Tennessee. They were also quite productive as hunters and weather forecasters, in the tradition of Bram.

The arm of the family descending from Bram came from a hardy bunch of Dutch cats. Amsterdam has a very friendly environment for cats; basically, we own that city. Cats were accustomed to sailing up and down the canals of Amsterdam, and Bram's sailing experience was extensive before he boarded the ship that brought him to the United States. Bram's sailing expertise and his commanding nature had made him the natural choice for Captain's Assistant.

My ancestors come from a wide variety of backgrounds, cultures, and breeds, and thanks to meowcestry.cat, I have been able to track down much of my heritage. My name, Fleur-de-Lys, is French, which is appropriate since some of my ancestors are Chartreux. I have the thick, blue-grey fur and gold eyes typical of Chartreux cats. My solid body and long legs are also traits, as is my happy smile.

My personality characteristics also give away my Chartreux heritage. I am friendly, playful, and confident, and I enjoy travel. When my mother opens my carrier, I walk in without hesitation because this usually means a vacation. I am treated like royalty at hotels with a special sign on the door for four-legged guests.

My Chartreux ancestors were easy to track since they came from French royalty. My long-ago, many greats grandfather, Alain, was stolen from his castle by a Huguenot because of his extraordinary hunting abilities. During his time in the castle, Alain had gained a reputation as an extraordinary hunter of mice, birds, insects, and other critters. One of the castle servants was a Huguenot, and, naturally, he recognized Alain's talents. Therefore, when this servant sailed to America with Jean Ribald and the Huguenots, he absconded with Alain.

Descendants from both my Dutch ancestors and my French ancestors settled in Rogersville, and the two families had many traits in common. Cats from both families were adventurous with strong, adaptable personalities. Many strong, happy kittens resulted from these two extraordinary cat branches. One such descendant, with both Dutch and French heritage, was Boot. During the late 1850s and 1860s, Boot lived in Rogersville, Tennessee where he met Golden, a beautiful red-gold cat with tabby markings. Golden possessed a joie de vivre that brought happiness to every creature she met.

Boot's people were Fred and Alice. They lived in a comfortable home on the outskirts of Rogersville. Fred and Alice grew wonderful orchards filled with an abundance of fruit trees—apples, pears, peaches, pawpaws, persimmons, mulberries. They also had gardens that were the envy of their neighbors. The farm was named Plum Hill. Boot's children patrolled the orchards and gardens daily, keeping pests at bay and giving weather reports to their people.

The harvests of Plum Hill were bountiful, as befitted the efforts and productivity of Fred, Alice, Boot, and Golden, and each was justly proud. Alice made delectable jellies and pies that were famous for miles around them.

Fred and Alice had twelve children; Boot and Golden had five playful kittens. Life was idyllic at Plum Hill for many years. In addition to running Plum Hill, Fred opened a printing company and printed books about Tennessee history and law. He also published the first newspaper in the region, and he was outspoken in his views against the evils of slavery. Fred was like a lion roaring his message about justice using the most powerful words he knew. Sometimes, Fred would even make up words to get his point across more forcefully. Fred became well-known in the community, and, eventually, he won political office as an ardent abolitionist.

Fred was tireless in his pursuits. He believed in the importance of education and started the first college in the area for females. He worked to develop stable banking practices so that individuals and businesses could borrow and grow. Under his influence, the first library in the area was opened. This library was funded by private citizens, but all citizens in the area were invited to use the library resources. Fred's life and the life of the townspeople during this time could have been halcyon.

The 1860s, however, were years of tremendous upheaval and sadness all over our country. And Rogersville was right at the crossroads of this chaos.

This was a period of deep divisions in the way that people thought and lived. As the children of Fred and Alice grew up, they became independent, and they developed opinions of their own—opinions that diverged from those of Fred and Alice. Or some of them did. As is common in families, people spoke their minds. At the dinner table, one son or daughter would voice an idea on one side of an issue and a sibling would disagree. These disagreements sometimes became very heated.

In spite of all the acrimony within the family, this was, in some ways, a good time for Boot and Golden and their

154

children. Because of the arguments around the Plum Hill dining table, proper table manners were not observed, and food often ended up on the floor. These humans would growl and hiss at each other with claws out and ears back. Fur would fly. Sometimes to the delight of Boot and Golden, globs of mashed potatoes, green beans, carrots, peas, corn, chunks of meat, biscuits, and pieces of cornbread would land on the floor. The cats would position themselves under the table ready to devour this bounty. It was an upside-down world.

When humans cannot argue their way into resolving a difference, they resort to violence. Cats are actually much more subtle and imaginative. Yeah, I know we have cat fights, but hissing and growling usually does the trick. With humans, if they can't beat their opponents with words, they just try to beat them up. In his writing, Fred called this argumentum ad baculum—argument of the club or cudgel. (Fred was a Latin scholar, in addition to all of his other accomplishments.) Fred pointed out over and over that argumentum ad baculum was a logical fallacy, but people were ignoring logic.

Tennessee seceded from the Union in 1861—the last state to join the Confederacy. East Tennessee was a stronghold of Union loyalties. And so it was in families. Living in East Tennessee, Fred and Alice were strong Union proponents, along with five of their children. Fred had actively lobbied to remain with the Union. Two of their children were supportive of the Confederacy. The remaining children were just very sad about all of this division. It was a tragic period.

The people in the town of Rogersville, like Fred's and Alice's family, were divided in their loyalties as states went into battle with one another. When the Union Army marched into the town, the Union soldiers stayed at the Hale Springs Inn. When the Confederate Army showed up, the Confederate soldiers stayed across the street at another hotel. (Thankfully, these troops were not staying at the hotels simultaneously.)

Alice spent hours trying to prepare good meals for her family, and her work was made more difficult because food was scarce. Union blockades of the waterways successfully impeded food supplies to Southerners. Alice was able to grow fruit in her orchards throughout most of the war, but she shared food with the starving soldiers and townspeople. Then, from the small amounts of food left, Alice diligently prepared meals for her family, wanting to pull them together. During a meal, though, one sibling invariably would push a hot button; another would invariably take the bait. Fur would fly. With her head in her hands, Alice would sit at her table in sadness, even though her mother had drilled into her about keeping her elbows off the table. Niceties just didn't matter during this period. Soon, one or more siblings would storm off in anger. Fred would usually just slam his fist on the table and then go back to venting in his newspaper column. And so it was at dining tables in most of Rogersville.

Boot and Golden, being pragmatic parents, trained their children to behave accordingly. During this period, the cats would move under the table from one sibling or parent to another favoring the one with the best treats.

As sons died in the War, families' attitudes further hardened. Neighbors refused to speak to one another when they disagreed with the other's war stance. During one of the Rogersville stays by the Confederate Army, Fred and other Union sympathizers were asked to swear an oath of allegiance to the Confederacy. When Fred refused, he was jailed. During Fred's imprisonment, Alice and some of the children faithfully visited him, while the Southern loyalists in his family ignored him in his jail cell. As it turned out, one of the Confederacy's commanding officers had worked in Fred's printing company, and he had Fred released from jail after four weeks.

Four of Fred's and Alice's children were killed during the Civil War. Fred became a changed person after the loss of his sons. He no longer had the inclination to publish opinions against either of the opposing sides. He and Alice maintained their home and orchards at Plum Hill as well as they could. When the war ended, Fred and Alice lived quietly secluded along with their remaining family.

After the loss to the Union, Confederate soldiers returned home to their families. They were tattered and defeated in more ways than one. The pro-Union townspeople had very little feelings of elation because of the great sadness of losing family, friends, and neighbors. The pro-Confederate townspeople just buried their heads and made themselves scarce in public affairs. It was a grey, bitter time.

Then, as often happens, a person wakes up one morning and it is springtime, with flowers blooming and birds chirping, and life seems promising. So it was with Fred and Alice. Their children married, and grandchildren were running around all over Plum Hill. Kittens climbing the fruit trees were followed by laughing grandchildren. One of Fred and Alice's sons became mayor of the town, and another became a judge. Fred and Alice's children opened thriving businesses in Rogersville—a milling business, a bank, a hardware store. Their children bought acres of land nearby and started farms. One son had inherited the adventurer genes from past generations and he took off for California to join an uncle who had gone in search of gold with the "49ers".

Plum Hill became alive again with birthday celebrations, sleigh rides, Easter egg hunts, July 4 festivities, Halloween costume parties, Thanksgiving feasts, Christmas holidays. Life at Plum Hill was busy and full again. Occasionally, a smile could even be glimpsed on Fred's solemn face.

Fred was a proud, imposing person—a veritable lion. His life had been filled with success prior to the war. Now the war had ended. His side had won. But some of his children and many of his friends had died. For Fred, it was not a time of victory, but of great loss, instead.

As a cat, the complexity of humans confounds me. On the one hand, they are willing to give their lives for people they've never met, but they fight against the people they love most. I have seen it during all of the eras in which my

157

relatives found themselves with this confusing species. Humans seem to be a naturally invasive species, riding into a new environment and taking over the situation. We felines adjust and live in harmony within our environment and the other dwellers in our habitat. We meow loudly to let our feelings be known, but we don't feel the need to kill off those we disagree with just to prove a point. Humans come along and try to control their surroundings, and they often worsen things for all of us.

I feel a great sense of kinship to Fred. Both of us are lovers of words. My ancestors who lived with Fred were inspired by his pioneer spirit in publishing newspapers and writing his ideas for all to read. That inspiration has traveled through the generations for more than 170 years to my paws so that I can tell my tales.

While I was cogitating, I heard my staff opening the door.

"Hello, Fleur-de-Lys! What did you do while we were away? Did you take a cat nap?" (My staff is always amused by this tired line.)

"Oh! Look at this! Fleur-de-Lys has left us a toy mouse on top of the computer. She must have written a story."

Whenever my staff leaves, I place a mouse for them in a strategic spot in our home. When I place my Tropical Mouse (it is orange and yellow) near my food bowl, the staff realize this is a hint. Often, I put my red, white and blue Liberty Mouse near the doorway as a friendly greeting. Today, I had placed Noel Mouse (red and green) near the computer because I had prepared a gift for them—a story to read.

This is a story that needs to be told about long-ago people living during a tragic period of conflict in the history of this country. Brothers, sisters, friends, and neighbors turned against one another, families were split apart, and many people died. It is also a story about the town that was divided itself. When the war ended, it is said that neighbors walked on the side of the street that indicated where their sympathies lay during the war.

My ancestors, Bram, Boot, and Golden were bigger-than-life cats. They were adventurers and hard workers. I am very proud of my ancestry, and I am proud of their persevering staff, Fred and Alice.

In the evenings, after his writing was finished and the work around Plum Hill was done for the day, Fred would sit in his chair and talk with Boot and Golden and their children. They didn't have television back in those days, and Fred would entertain everyone with his stories. To Boot and Golden, Fred was a giant cat, lion-like, ferociously defending his family, roaring his strong beliefs about equality and liberty and justice through his powerful words. Almost every evening, Fred also reminded his listeners that cats were superior to humans because they didn't engage in wars, among other reasons. Fred recognized what I've been trying to convey to my staff for years.

THE END

About the Authors

Ellen Redd and Fleur-de-Lys

Ellen Redd lives in Marco Island with her husband and their cat, Fleur-de-Lys. Ellen retired from engineering software and editing computer and accounting books. She enjoys playing piano and assisting organizations that support animals.

Fleur-de-Lys Redd is a grey cat person with gold eyes and a friendly smile. Fleur-de-Lys is polydactyl with thumbs on her front feet and extra toes on all four feet. Fleur-de-Lys also enjoys playing piano and engaging in a wide variety of sports with her capable paws.

The Era of the Publishing Lion is a product of Fleur-de-Lys' vivid imagination, but some of the historical elements in her story are based in actual events.

HOME WAS RE-DEFINED BY AN AIRPLANE COLLISION

Joanne Ivy Stankievich, © 2010

Thursday evening:
"Our home is perfect!" I comment to Walter, after painting our entry closet—the last effort to make the Brooklyn apartment into our home. It's a one bedroom, third floor walk-up apartment in a row-house on Seventh Avenue, just a block in from busy Flatbush Avenue.

I think back to growing up on our family farm during the Depression and war years: many of the farm furnishings were sturdy, but second-hand. My mother's taste in decorating went toward flowery curtains and wallpaper with wobbly designs.

How proud I am, now, to have a home of my own, furnished in my style. The new walnut, Scandinavian-look furniture has such clean, straight lines. And the neutral beige on the walls sets off the contemporary abstract green and orange living room curtains just right. It's exactly what I've always wanted my home to be like.

Late morning, Friday, December 16, 1960
I finish my breakfast in the kitchen, looking out over the sturdy concrete block church on the street behind our apartment building. I'm due to start work at 2 p.m. at the Green Point Housing Authority as part of my graduate school social work assignment, so I quickly finish eating and go into the bathroom for a shower.

161

Stepping out of the shower, I hear a piercing, too close rumble. *That plane sure sounds like it's flying too low!* That is my last thought before the thunderous crash.

The whole building is swaying sharply from one side to the other, back and forth, back and forth. I grab the bathroom sink to hold myself upright. The heavy wire grate on the bathroom ceiling comes loose and flies toward me.

I lower my head and close my eyes to mentally shut out what seems my impending death. I plead out loud, "God, help me!" I sense myself being encompassed by bright light. Then I become calm, feeling the assurance of God's loving presence and care. At that point, it doesn't seem to matter to me whether I stay on earth or leave it. There is a realization that life—for me and for the others involved in whatever this is—is continuously on-going. Although I don't know how, I feel certain that it is true.

Suddenly, the building stops swaying. As I open the bathroom door, I'm struck by searing heat. Looking toward the back, I see two chairs near shattered windows bursting into flames like tinder in a fireplace. Flames are leaping up my frothy dining room curtains; in fact, the whole wall is ablaze. The now windowless opening at the back reveals open space where the steepled church had been just moments before.

I dash out of the apartment door to escape down the stairs. But as I reach the first step, I see the young couple running down from the attic apartment above and realize I'm naked, having just gotten out of the shower. *I can't go out on the street like this!* With concern for my safety, but definitely not wanting to be seen naked in public, I run back into the apartment to quickly put on my nightgown and grab my purse.

Back down the stairs, I enter the snow-covered street in my bare feet and flimsy nightgown. The chaos of the scene overwhelms me: people running and screaming, or just standing there, paralyzed with the horror of it all.

"What happened?" I ask a woman who is standing nearby, with tears in her eyes.

"An airliner crashed into the intersection. I don't think anyone could have survived."

How horrible, I think; *all those people and their families!* It seems incomprehensible.

I gaze toward the intersection. Over the heads of onlookers, I see pieces of jagged metal littering the nearby cross streets; the word United is written across one large piece. Flames leap toward the sky; smoke fills my eyes and lungs with its acidity. Whistles and sirens blare: fire engines, ambulances, and police are beginning to converge on the scene.

I begin to shiver. I look down at my bare feet in the snow and then feel concerned about people seeing through my thin nightie. The white-haired lady from the dry cleaners down the street sees my plight and realizes I've just escaped the burning building. She gently places a left-over coat around my shoulders for protection from the still falling snow. A passer-by bends over to take plastic booties off her shoes and hands them to me to cover my feet. Tears of gratitude well in my eyes for such kindnesses. I can't speak, but give each a hug.

I'm wandering, probably in shock, unable to move beyond my own experience. I'm trying to grasp my situation, thinking: *All I have left in this world is my nightie and purse.*

My thought clarifies: *Forget about going to work. What should I do? Call Walter and ask him to come back from his job in New Jersey.* I walk around the corner to the newspaper store to use the pay phone. Before picking up the telephone, I consciously calm myself. With a voice forced under

---

[1]Later, I learn that two airliners collided over Staten Island in a heavy snowstorm, with the greater part of the one airliner hurtling onto the intersection of Seventh Ave and Sterling Place, Brooklyn—our closest intersection. The tail section of that plane pierced the roof of our building, evidently, the tremendous force of it was what caused the swaying and destabilizing.

control, I dial and say, "Walter, a plane has hit our apartment; I think you should come home."

"Well," his logical reply is, "why don't you call the fire department. I don't see any reason to leave work early; there's nothing I can do about it."

What? I think, with exasperation. *What a typical engineering attitude!* Usually I appreciate his calm, no-problem response to situations, but not this time. He obviously doesn't understand. I finally lose control, excitedly exclaiming, "Walter, I have no clothes and no place to go; the whole city's emergency vehicles are already at the site. You'd better start back RIGHT NOW! I'll meet you around the corner in the Reading Room."

By now, reporters are converging on the area. One yells into the store, "Did anyone see what happened?" I hesitate. No, I decide. Mine might be a good first-person story for him, but I can't let my thought dwell on that scene of death and destruction right now. It would be too overwhelming to rehash what I'd just been through. My current fragile mental state just couldn't handle it.

I need a quiet place to calm my thought. With gratitude for its close proximity on Sterling Place, I seek the haven of the nearby Christian Science Reading Room.

"What happened to you?" the attendant asks, seeing my strange attire and frazzled look.

"The airplane hit our apartment. I need some time to just sit quietly and read and pray until my husband arrives." It will soon be closing time, but the attendant kindly offers to stay open another hour or so until Walter arrives from New Jersey. I can see that she has her head down and is probably quietly praying about the whole situation.

I walk past the bookstore portion of the Reading Room into the glass-enclosed study room so that I can collect my thoughts: I need to replace the distressing scene that I've just left with a spiritual uplift. I pick up the book, *Science and*

Health,[2] and let it fall open. The page includes a definition of substance from a spiritual standpoint: "Substance is that which is eternal and incapable of discord and decay." It strikes me clearly that this can be applied to home: the real substance of home isn't the building or the material things we put into the building. The important aspects of home have to do with the indestructible qualities we bring to that location: outreaching love in hospitality to others, harmony in considerate spousal relationships, and beautiful thoughts that would naturally be reflected in beautiful surroundings.

Now that I have been reminded of what is truly important in life, the mental imprint of the burning apartment isn't so significant.

Walter and I are intact. I rejoice, thinking that this new perspective of home can be carried with us wherever we might live—whether or not there is anything left of our newly purchased furnishings.

I'm grateful for something good to hold onto in the midst of such turmoil.

Walter finally arrives, looking a bit sheepish about his first response, as he notes the pervasive destruction of the nearby scene.

"Hon, I'm so sorry about my stupid response when you called. I was thinking about the commuter buses not operating in the middle of the day, and that I'd have to ask a colleague to take time off work to drive me into Brooklyn. Until we heard about the crash on the car radio, I couldn't really comprehend the situation."

Although I'm usually a take charge person, after all that has just happened, I am now relieved to have my quieter, even-keeled husband present, taking over responsibility for the next decisions. He ushers me out the door and back down the street, around the smoking debris, and toward our building. All the fires seem to be out, most emergency

---

[2] *Science and Health with Key to the Scriptures* by Mary Baker Eddy p468, 17-18

‾vehicles have left, and now there are mainly police guarding the roped off area.

"We live in this building. Can we go in to get some belongings?" Walter asks a policeman in front of our apartment building.

"No, we have to determine how stable the building is first, which might take several days. You'll have to check back later."

What are we going to do? Where can we go? I know we don't have any extra money in our bank account: we just overspent on furnishing our apartment. I feel disoriented again.

Walter calls his parents and finds they have an unoccupied rental room in their apartment building where we can stay for a few days. We realize, also, we may have to start looking for a new apartment—hopefully, one we can immediately move in whatever may be left of our furnishings.

The next need is to buy other clothing than what I am wearing: the flimsy nightgown, booties and borrowed coat. Getting to the car, parked a few blocks away, driving roundabout all the closed off streets, we make our way to the A & S department store in downtown Brooklyn. I purchase underwear, stockings, shoes, some makeup, and finally a dress.

The clerk says, "Let me wrap that up for you."

"That's OK; I'll just wear it out."

"Fine, I'll wrap up the dress you wore in," the clerk responds.

I'm quiet for a moment. I really don't want to have to go into details about why she can't do that since, by then, I am beginning to feel a little shaky. The impact of what has happened, not only to us, but to all the others involved in the crash, is just beginning to be grasped.

Feeling humiliated, I finally blurt out, "I'm sorry, you can't do that. I didn't wear any in to the store." Although I don't want to talk about what happened, I'm forced to explain: "We've been burned out in the airplane crash."

After we arrive at Walter's parents' building, I excuse myself from their dining room and go into our rental room to collapse and be alone. The immensity of the situation has finally hit: those hundreds who'd died in the planes and on the ground! Only then can I turn thought away from my own personal situation and toward the larger picture. I pray that God's loving and comforting embrace may be felt by the grieving relatives and all those affected by this horrific plane collision.

- - - - -

A few days later, our apartment building was deemed to be stable enough for us to gather our belongings. Unfortunately, it was not habitable, so we did need to find a new place to live. As it turned out, most of our belongings were retrievable. The firemen had chosen our apartment from which to fight the flames; thus, it was secured quickly.

When we first entered the shambles of our apartment, I noted that the pans on the kitchen stove had melted flat. I realized that, if the crash had been ten minutes earlier, it would have caught me having breakfast in that kitchen and I probably would have been incinerated. Instead, I was in the windowless bathroom, which protected me from the blast of the imploding church behind our apartment.

For us, there was some good that eventually came from this experience. It became an opportunity to rethink job options for both of us, as well as living locale. "What is it we really want out of life?" I asked. This was a little deeper than I'd been thinking before, with the excitement of a wedding and establishing a new home. Part of the answer that came back was: a quieter community in which to raise a family in the future. This began a shift for us from city life to the suburbs.

The lessons learned about what home really is—the qualities we bring to the house—were applied with increasingly happy results to our next twenty moves, the majority in foreign countries, with various kinds of furnishings.

About the Author

Joanne Ivy Stankievich

Joanne Ivy Stankievich currently lives in Naples, Florida, though she recently lived in New Jersey and Europe: Munich, Prague, and Florence.

She is the author of the historical memoir, "LIVING WITH A SCENT OF DANGER, European Adventures at the Fall of Communism." The book is about Stankievich's and her husband Walter's, experiences while participating in events around the fall of the Iron Curtain, when he worked for the Belarus Service of Radio Free Europe/Radio Liberty.

The story shared here happened to her in 1960 and is included in a book she is writing: "BEYOND MY BORDERS, from Covered Wagons to Driverless Cars." It is a collection of memoir essays about turning points of a family from pioneer times to today. This experience was definitely a 'turning point.'

Miracle on Cape Romano

Joanne Simon Tailele

The tumultuous fury raging in Patrice Cummings' belly matched the chop of the sea as she steered her twenty-six-foot Hurricane deck boat out of Caxambas Pass. "Why does he have to be such a pompous ass?" She glanced at the foreboding sky quickly gaining strength from the east and pushed the throttle to maximum knots. The anger boiling in her gut squashed any sense of reason. If she had any luck, she'd make it to Goodland through Coon Key Pass before the storm was upon her.

She was not lucky.

"Damn, damn, damn," she muttered to herself as the rain pelted her from the starboard side. Being low tide when she boarded, going through Caxambas Bay was not a viable option. She would bottom out on the sand bars, even with her shallow draft. Going around the south-west side of Rice Island and Cape Romano was her only choice, and she would still have to watch for the shoals by the tip of the island while dealing with more open sea.

She shouted back at a thunderous Neptune as three-foot waves rocked the boat precariously port side. "He started it." Okay, even she had to admit that sounded childish. If only she could learn to control her temper. Why was it easier on the lobby floor in the State House than it was in her own living room?

She cursed Edward for making her angry enough to do such a stupid thing as take the boat out in a storm just to get away from him. The last five years had not been easy ones. Edward's thriving business as a respected eye surgeon, the first in Collier County, had dwindled down to a hand-full of clients. Younger, more current surgeons that specialized in laser surgery had all but run him out of business. This morning was the last straw. Edward quietly announced over soft-boiled eggs and toast that he was closing up shop. If that wasn't enough to ruin one's morning, he added that it was time to put their luxury home in the Estates of Marco Island on the market. He confessed to some bad investments that wiped out their savings and the only thing left to live on was the equity in the house. That is, what was left of the equity, after two cash-outs in refinancing and a new second mortgage.

Patrice chastised herself for having been allowed to be coddled into a false sense of security. Edward handled all the finances and she never questioned where the money was coming from before she took off on elaborate vacations or extended trips to Washington DC. Her passion was politics and she spent countless hours working for the Republican Party, lobbying for their issues and executing fundraisers. She single-handedly raised six hundred thousand dollars for the party with her efforts lobbying for tougher immigration laws. It was a drop in a bucket compared to what they needed to stop the liberal Democrats. Patrice was disgusted with the leniency of the past government that had not tightened the borders or deported illegal aliens. She and her new president had a lot of work to do. The illegal aliens used the American people's resources but didn't pay taxes. She refused to set foot in Miami where her best friend's daughter was killed in an auto accident by an illegal immigrant without a driver's license or insurance. Patrice was hell bent on shipping them all back to where they came from.

170

Her small boat was not equipped for stormy open seas. She was a good captain and could handle the boat as well as any man around Marco Island, but even Patrice had to admit that taking a small boat out in weather like this was foolish at best.

She spotted the white round roofline of the abandoned dome house of Cape Romano, poking out of the green sea like an alien spaceship. Perhaps the smartest thing to do was to anchor up to the partially submerged pilings until the storm passed. She turned toward the domes, hoping she wouldn't get stuck in the shoals dredged up from recent storms that deposited sand in the treacherous shallow waters along the coast. Patrice pulled alongside and tied the aft to the pilings. She dropped the anchor and tugged to bury it in the shoal to keep the bow from swinging around and crashing into the cement structure.

No one had lived on Cape Romano for decades, not since Mike Morgan, the grandson of Bob and Margaret Lee, the original owners and architects of the unusual structure fled for their lives when Hurricane Andrew came through in 1992. The dome home had once sat on dry land, far back from the beach, along with an A-frame and a Stilt house. The sea and Andrew collapsed the other structures and claimed most of island. Now, the infamous dome home of Cape Romano was all that was left, and it sat partially submerged in the Gulf of Mexico.

Drenched and cold from the gusts of wind on her wet body, Patrice struggled to pull herself into one of the concrete dwellings. Two of the domes had already shifted away from the others and were leaning precariously in the water. In another circumstance, she would have taken the time to appreciate the strange architecture; futuristic, mushroom shaped rooms once joined together by cat-walks. But not today.

She heard a shrill cry.

"Oooowwwhhhhooo. Aaaahhhhrrrr."

She crouched down behind the graffitied column. What could it be? Could the wind make an eerie sound like that?

171

She looked around for another boat. Maybe it was a confrontation between drug dealers going terribly wrong. No boat in site. Or . . . as unusual as it would be for a Florida panther to be out in the water, they could swim. It was entirely possible it got stranded after a particularly low tide and was now trapped in the building. Boaters were famous for leaving leftovers from their parties in the abandoned structure. If a panther was hungry enough to swim here attracted by the smell of food, it could now be very hungry and very dangerous.

The sound echoed through the walls again. Whatever it was, it was in one of the other domes, a stone's throw from where she crouched.

"Oooowwwhhhhooo. Aaaahhhhrrrr."

The shrill scream sent a shiver down her back. She reached in her hobo bag and pulled out the small Derringer It may not be lethal enough to take down a panther that was in full charge, but it could be enough to deter it or let her get several rounds off if it was injured. She was grateful that, at least for now, her right to bear arms in the Second Amendment had not been taken away. She needed shelter also and was not about to share it with an angry hundred-pound cat.

Moving slowly forward, she stretched her arm in front of her, the small pistol in her hand. The sound came again, but in rapid succession.

"Oooowwwhhhhooo, Aaaahhhhrrrr, ayeeeaaahhhrrr, Oooowwwhhhhooo, Aaaahhhhrrrr Oooowwwhhhhooo."

Then another sound took her totally by surprise. A human voice. "*Por favor,* push, the *bebé,* it is coming now."

Patrice only understood a miniscule amount of Spanish, but she recognized "*Por favor*" as please and "*bebé*" as baby. *Baby? Is someone in there having a baby? Here?* Was it possible that the sound she heard was not a panther, but a woman in labor? On this deserted concrete dome island?

She crept closer to the adjoining dome and peered through the open window frame. On the concrete floor, a young girl in rags lay with her legs splayed open, knees raised as a bedraggled, dark haired, young man crouched in front of her. Crystals of salt water clung to the girl's dark hair and tears streaked down her cheeks. She had bitten her lip until it bled crimson against her brown cheeks. The boy's back was to Patrice but his shoulders shook as if he was also crying. He ripped off his shirt and laid it between her legs, ready to accept the baby.

The girl looked up and saw Patrice peering in the window. With her blonde hair plastered against her skull, her skin as white as snow, she must have looked like an apparition.

The girl screamed. *"Fantasma!"*

The young man misunderstood. "No, no. No ghost. You are going to be fine. The bebé . . . it is almost here."

"Si, Raul, si."

Patrice watched her point toward the window where she was frozen in place.

The boy turned and gasped, throwing his body over the girl, trying to protect her from whatever apparition was coming through the window.

Patrice jumped from her knees below the window and ran to the doorway. "No!" She screamed "I won't hurt you. I promise."

The couple on the floor clutched each other and scooted across the floor on their behinds.

Between the girl's legs, Patrice could see the round shape of a head crowning. She rushed to their side but they shrieked in fright. "The bebé . . . be . . . bebé . . . it is coming." She rocked her arms to indicate a baby. She meant no harm, but when she realized she still had the Derringer in her hand quickly dropped it into her pocket. She raised her hands, the universal sign for submission. "See, I won't hurt you. I can help." She tried to move closer and again they scooted away from her.

She knelt down in front of them and opened her hands, palms up. "Por favor. Let me help."

The girl let out another scream and Patrice took over. She was grateful for the Red Cross classes she had recently completed. By no means a doctor, but she did practice birthing procedures with a Cabbage Patch doll. She rested her hand on the bent knee and reached between the girl's legs. She guided the head through the opening and turned the child so her shoulders could be freed. The umbilical cord was wrapped around the infant's neck, so Patrice gently untangled it. She pulled the clip from her hair and clamped off the cord. "Knife, do you have a knife to cut the cord?"

The young man looked at her in confusion. She made scissor-like motions with her fingers, hoping he would understand.

"Ah, *Si, si.*" He pulled a fishing knife from his belt. It was not sanitary by any means, but Patrice had no other choice. The first-aid kit on her boat had sterile supplies, but there was not time to try to explain. She folded the umbilical cord in two and sliced through it with the fishing knife. Then she took the shirt lying on the concrete floor and wiped the blood smears off the baby girl. She was not crying. This was not good. She probed her finger into the child's mouth and removed the mucous blocking her airway. She held the child upside down by the feet, slapping it gently on her back. "Come on, baby, breathe." The bundle jerked in her hand and let out a squeaky cry. She shouted out in joy along with the parents. Patrice gently laid the child on the mother's chest and backed away, giving the couple a few moments to share their joy in private.

The man bent down and kissed his wife, then his new baby girl. Tears streamed down his face. He looked over at Patrice. "*Gracias, muchas gracias.*"

Patrice smiled back, her angry thoughts about Edward or her political agenda on immigration forgotten, at least for now.

A bolt of lightning quickly followed by a huge clap of thunder startled the child that flinched in her mother's arms and wailed. What a noisy world she had just come in to.

***

Patrice leaned back on her haunches and observed the new family. Where had they come from? How did they get there? There was no boat in sight. Did they live on Goodland or Marco? In her gut, Patrice knew the answer was no. They were "those people," the ones she lobbied so hard to have shipped back to wherever, or imprisoned for breaking United States immigration laws. But they looked nothing like the images she had carried around in her head. These two of "those people" didn't look like drug dealers or undesirables. They looked like scared, young children, now with a child of their own, an American citizen, born on American soil. Well, kind of—on American waters. What should Patrice do now?

Well, first things first. She had to get them to safety, and the mother and child to a hospital. She'd deal with the correct political decisions later. Patrice looked at the stormy sea. It still raged and there was no way they could take her small boat out in this weather. She could call the Coast Guard. They'd come in a bigger boat, and they'd handle the problems of getting them to safety. She reached into her back pocket for her cell phone. The young man lunged toward her and knocked the phone from her hand. It skidded across the concrete floor, slipped through the opening for a door and into the water.

Patrice groaned. "Help," she said. "I needed to call for help. My boat isn't big enough to get through this storm." Did they understand a word she was saying?

He shook his head. "*No policia.*" His eyes spoke more than his words. They pleaded with her, searching in her eyes for her heart. A glimmer of compassion. "Por favor."

Wasn't that what she was trying to do? Get them someplace safe? A hospital for his wife and child. But she knew what his real fear was—deportation—that they would be sent back from wherever they came from. Which was exactly what she would have sworn was the right thing to do yesterday, before helping to bring that small bundle into the world. Right now, it all looked so different: They were no longer nameless, faceless immigrants. These were people, with hopes and dreams and love for each other and love for their child.

Patrice nodded. Okay, no police. No Coast Guard. But she couldn't just leave them there, on a concrete dome surrounded by sea water with no food, no fresh water, no true shelter. She shivered, suddenly aware of her own wet body, hair stringing down her back. One look at her dripping wet black J. Crew boy shorts, chartreuse Zella tank-top and Nike boat shoes and it was obvious, not only to her, but to the young couple in rags before her, that theirs were worlds apart. She settled back into the corner. Once the storm let up, she'd figure something out.

"Patrice," she said, pointing to herself. At least they could find out each other's names. Who knew how long they would have to wait out this storm.

The young mother timidly smiled. "Pilar." She tapped a slender finger to her chest. "Raul," she pointed to her husband. She looked down at the child, wrapped in a colorful shawl, pulled close to her chest and shrugged.

"Maria Isabella Teresa Rojas," Raul raised his chin and spoke proudly.

Patrice laughed out load. "That is quite a long name for such a tiny little girl. May I simply call her Maria?"

"Si, Maria," Pilar answered. "Hold . . . would you like hold?"

Patrice was unnerved by the question. She couldn't remember the last time she held an infant. The Richardson children had been grown and on their own for years. And no grand-children—yet. It would be nice to hold a little one. Yes, Patrice nodded and stretched out her arms.

Pilar handed the curly-haired infant to Raul, who placed her in Patrice's arms. The child blinked, and stared with dark eyes that seem to suck in her very soul. So innocent, so trusting. Patrice felt her heart melting. She had to do what was right for this innocent new soul. Was everything she had so ardently believed been wrong? The responsibility of three innocent lives weighed heavy on her heart.

When Raul placed Maria back in Pilar's arms, she began to softly sing. *"Arrurru mi niña* (Lull to sleep my daughter*)"* The child nuzzled into Pilar's chest, and instantly grabbed on to the offered breast, suckling noisily.

***

By sunset, the storm had passed and Patrice was anxious to get home before dark. Edward would be looking for her. Surely, there would have been numerous messages from him on her cell phone by now—if her cell phone wasn't on the bottom of the Gulf of Mexico.

Patrice wished she had the phone and could let Edward know she was all right. He'd be worried by now. What had they been arguing about so violently? Oh yes, him giving up the business, squandering their life savings, wanting to sell the house. A flicker of anger raised its ugly head until she looked over at the new family. None of that seemed important anymore compared to what had happened in the last several hours.

Patrice looked at Raul, Pilar and Maria. This would be quite the surprise when she showed up with her new friends.

***

Edward was waiting when Patrice turned the boat into the lift. He was pacing the length of the dock, eyes searching for her. She waved when he spotted them. He was not smiling. He was angry. She could see it from there. Was he still angry about what they had argued about, or about her taking his precious boat out in the storm?

She loved how his hair was bleached almost white from hours in the Florida sun and his broad tanned shoulders flexed when she tossed him the tie ropes. He wouldn't meet her eyes as he tied up to the cleats.

"Where the hell have you been? I've been . . ."

Patrice watched his brows knit together and his perfect lips form an O when Raul and Pilar stepped from the cabin, a small bundle in Pilar's arms.

"Edward, this is Raul and Pilar and little Maria."

"Um . . . um." She had rarely seen him speechless. He stared at the couple, then back at Patrice.

Patrice yanked on his arm, "Ed, where are your manners? Give Pilar some help out of the boat. Can't you see she has her hands full?"

"Oh, yes, yes. I'm sorry." He reached for Pilar's arm and helped her step onto the dock. Then he reached a hand to Raul.

The men gripped hands, half suspended between the boat and the dock. Patrice noticed the contrast of their hands, one soft and fair, even with a suntan, the other dark and coarse. They came from such different worlds.

Patrice took over. "Okay now, let's get everyone up to the house. We could all use some dry clothes and decent food." She ushered her guests up the pavers, through the screened lanai with expansive pool and spa, into the elegant twenty-foot high coffered great room. "The guest wing is this way." She headed to the left, expecting them to follow.

Raul and Pilar held back, mouths gaped open taking in the sparkling pool, the expansive rooms, the Robb and Stucky décor. For the first time in her life, Patrice was embarrassed by all the opulence, a departure from her normal feeling of pride. The home was surely like nothing they had ever seen.

Patrice fumbled with her wet blouse. "Come now. I'm sure Pilar can fit into some of my clothes and although they may be a bit large, Edward can spare some things for you, Raul." She looked at the baby. "When I get changed, I'll run to the store and pick up some things for Maria, diapers, and onesies, and receiving blankets."

Pilar looked embarrassed too, and dropped her chin to her chest, cooing at the infant.

Once Patrice found them some clothes and showed them how to work the rain shower, she left them alone in the guest suite to clean up. Edward was waiting for her in the master suite.

"Wow! I'm blown away. You leave in a fit of anger, jump fool-heartedly into a boat in the middle of a storm and come back hours later with *them?* I don't even know where to begin with my questions. Wherever did you find them? Who are they?"

"They were in the domes. And Pilar was in labor. Edward, I helped give birth to that baby! Can you believe it? It was the most wondrous thing I've ever seen."

"You—you—who gets sick at the sight of blood, helped birth that baby?"

"Yes, Thank God I took that Red Cross class. I didn't even faint. And I couldn't just leave them there. What was I to do? So I brought them here." She dropped down beside him on the king-size bed as she peeled wet clothes from her body.

"The domes? As in Cape Romano?"

Patrice nodded.

"Shouldn't you call the authorities? You know they must be illegal immigrants. But how did they get to Cape Romano? Did they have a boat?"

"No, they had nothing. I don't know their story yet. But I had to . . . I have to help them."

"This is so unlike you, Patrice. I don't get it. You are harboring illegals, you do know that, don't you?"

Patrice shrugged. "I know. But I can't do it. These people have done nothing wrong. They just want a better life for themselves and their baby."

Edward wrapped his arms around his wife. "I'm proud of you, sweetheart. You never cease to amaze me. And frustrate me. And thrill me. About our fight. I'm sorry about our fight . . . and the house, the investments. I thought I was doing something good . . . until it all back-fired on me. I was so worried when you didn't come right back. I had all kinds of horrible visions about you being hurt or the boat capsizing or you drowning. I was afraid I lost you forever."

Patrice melted into the warmth of his arms. "I'm sorry too. I know you'd never intentionally do anything to jeopardize our family. We don't need this big house. We'll figure something out."

Edward kissed the top of her head. "What are we going

to do about our house guests? Do you plan on hiding them out here in our guest suite forever?"

"Of course not, silly. She pulled away and kissed his cheek. "I think the first thing I need to do, after a good hot shower, is fix them a hot meal. Then we can work on who they are, how they got here, and how to get them a visa so they don't get deported."

***

Patrice tapped lightly on the door to the guest suite. A soft voice bade her to come in. The young Rojas family was bundled together on the king-sized bed. Pilar was asleep, wrapped in Patrice's plush pink bathrobe, the baby swaddled in a fluffy bath towel in her arms. Raul lay beside them dressed in plaid flannel pajama bottoms that covered his feet and a too-large white T-shirt. His eyes barely held open, but he tried to rise when she entered.

"No, no, don't get up. You all need your rest. I'm going to the store. Anything special I can get you?" Did he understand anything that she was saying? Patrice gently pressed on his shoulder and he didn't resist as he lay back on the pillow. She pulled the comforter from the foot of the bed, covered the young family and tip-toed out of the room.

At the Walmart on Rt. 951, Patrice cruised up and down the baby department aisles. She piled diapers, onesies, footed sleepers, soft, downy baby blankets into the cart. There was Johnson's baby powder, and baby wash and shampoo. She tossed in a few pacifiers and bottles. She mused over the menagerie of equipment. Should she buy a car seat, a crib, stroller? *No*, she told herself. *They won't be with us that long.* Maybe just a port-a-crib and the car seat. She knew they couldn't go anywhere in the car without that.

Down the ladies aisles, she guessed on sizes, settling for things that ran small, medium, large rather than numbered sizes. Pilar was most definitely a small. Patrice picked out soft warm-ups, knee-length yoga pants, spandex shorts and a half dozen pretty cotton tops. She guessed on size 5 packages of cotton panties and size 32 nursing bras.

She repeated her guesswork for Raul in the men's department and headed for the check-out.

Constance Reading from her mahjong club cornered her in the waiting line. "Well hello, Patrice. We missed you last week. Were you back in Washington again? I can't keep up with you." Her glance traveled down to the items in Patrice's basket. "Baby items? What is all this? Are you going to be a grandmother?"

Patrice wanted to slink away without answering her. Constance Reading spent more time spreading the latest Marco Island gossip than she did playing her tiles on Wednesday mornings. The last thing Patrice wanted to do was let her know about her house guests.

"No." Patrice forced a laugh. "My daughter Amy's best friend is having a baby. Just getting some things to send for the shower."

Constance's smile turned downward. Nothing juicy here to share. She glanced again at the pile of men's and women's clothes, obviously nothing Patrice would ever wear. "I see. And are . . ."

Lucky for Patrice, the line moved forward, and because Constance had nothing to check out, the line forced her out of the way and away from Patrice.

***

Edward ushered a young man through the screened lanai and offered him a seat at the table of the outdoor kitchen. In the last ten years, as he had kept the Cumming's lawn perfectly manicured, he had never once been in the house or on the lanai. Patrice knew little about him, except that his family was from Miami, that his English was good, but he also spoke fluent Spanish.

Patrice set a tray with a pitcher of lemonade and glasses on the table in front of him. "Miguel, we need your help."

"Yes, ma'am."

"We're having a communication problem with our houseguests. We would greatly appreciate your service as an interpreter."

His eyes darkened, but he nodded. "Yes, ma'am. Okay, ma'am."

When Pilar and Raul stepped through the open doorway from the great room, Miguel started and began to rise. Edward placed his hand on his shoulder, and Miguel settled back in his seat.

"Miguel, I'd like you to meet Pilar and Raul Rojas," Patrice said.

"*Como esta?*" Miguel extended his hand and shook Raul's.

The young couple took a seat at the table. An awkward moment passed as the five sipped quietly on their lemonade.

Edward spoke first. "Miguel, Patrice found Raul and Pilar stranded in the dome homes on Cape Romano. I'm afraid we don't communicate well enough to know what happened to them. We were hoping you could talk to them and find out. We'd like to help them. Get them home, if that is what they want. Or help them find their family."

Miguel nodded. The conversation moved slowly at first. He'd ask one question, and get one word answers.

"Where are you from?"

"Columbia"

"Do you have a boat?

"No."

"Were you trying to come to America?

"Si."

Then the conversation took on a life of its own. Both parties spoke rapidly, the excitement and volume increasing with each response. Arms waved in demonstration. Patrice thought she understood part of it, like playing charades. Something about hiding and being tossed overboard. At one point, Raul gripped Pilar's hand as tears streamed down her face.

Edward and Patrice waited silently as the conversation reached its ebb and tide. As the story appeared to be winding down, baby Maria began to fuss in her port-a-crib. Pilar excused herself and slipped back into the house to tend to her daughter.

"It's quite a story," Miguel finally said to his employers. He looked at Raul, his eyes asking permission to share the story. Raul nodded.

"They are from Bolivar, Columbia. The ELN (National Liberation Army) guerillas took over his coffee plantation for coca cultivation. They forced them to grow and harvest the coca for cocaine production, then taxed them on the results. When some of his family resisted, they were shot on the spot. The violence in the area was increasing, even as the new president, Juan Manuel Santos, received the 2016 Nobel Peace Prize. Things became so bad they felt they had to escape. Getting a visa to come to America legally was impossible."

"Why?" Patrice had to ask.

"Not now," Edward chided. "Go on, Miguel. Finish the story."

"Raul and Pilar harvested the coca, processed it and moved it by truck to another location where they refined it into the powder that gets exported. After taxes, they didn't even make enough to live on." He paused and patted Raul's hand across the table.

"They covertly followed the shipment to the docks, paid every cent of what they had to let a sailor smuggle them aboard a coffee export ship that was covering the cocaine shipment. They hid in separate wooden barrels with nothing but two bottles of water each, for three days, never knowing if they would be discovered."

Patrice's hand flew to her mouth, imagining very pregnant Pilar stuffed into a wooden barrel, unable to see what was happening. The thought sickened her.

"Raul would talk to Pilar through the air holes in the barrels, encouraging her and telling her that they were going to make it. When the ship anchored three miles off-shore of southwest Florida to transfer the cocaine to smaller fishing boats, they had to take their chance then of getting onto the smaller boats. But they were discovered climbing out of the barrels."

Even though Patrice was looking at Raul and knew they had somehow made it, her first reaction was that they would have been killed, right there and then.

"Raul says that Pilar's faith in God saved them. She said that she prayed to the Virgin Mary and she knew she would save them. And she did. Instead of killing them, they threw them overboard."

"Because they were sure they would drown, right?" Edward asked.

"Right. But they didn't count on what a good swimmer Raul is. He followed the rising sun to the east and swam in that direction, pulling Pilar along with him as he went. He says he is not sure how many days he swam, but it was more than two nights. Then, just as his arms were giving out and he was sure they would drown, they saw land, and later the white dome roofs of Cape Romano. It gave him the stamina to keep going."

"Oh my God!" was all Patrice could muster.

"But the tide was low when they reached the dome house and he did not have the strength to pull himself or Pilar up. So they clung to the side of the pilings until the storm hit, and the tide came in. Then he was able to hoist Pilar through the openings and pull himself in behind her. He didn't know that Pilar was already in labor until she collapsed on the floor."

Patrice smiled now. "And then I showed up in my boat, scaring the living daylights out of them."

Raul nodded. That he understood.

Just hearing the story exhausted everyone, and for a few moments the only sound was that of Pilar, singing a Columbian lullaby to her daughter.

"Thank you, Miguel," Edward offered.

Miguel smiled. "My pleasure. I must get home to my family now." He turned to his new friend. "Raul is an amazing man. It is my pleasure to know him." He made his exit through the screen lanai door.

***

That evening, Patrice snuggled close to her husband, grateful for all the things she so often had taken for granted. Freedom to work as she chose, live without fear of persecution, the multitudes of material things surrounding her that no longer held the same brilliance.

"Babe, if it's the last thing I do in this world, I will find a way to get Raul and Pilar visas so they can stay here until they can go the legal route, and become US citizens."

Edward gave her a tight squeeze. "What about your lobby work on the wall? How are you going to justify that? Helping illegal aliens?"

"Edward, I think I just switched sides."

Cape Romano in 1992

About the Author

Joanne Simon Tailele

Joanne Simon Tailele grew up in Youngstown, Ohio. She wrote her first short story at ten years old. Her career in commercial fiction began in 2010 when she wrote her debut novel, *Accident*. She now has three women's fiction books, two biographies and one children's book to her name.

When she is not writing, she is editing and formatting manuscripts for other writers.

She is currently the secretary of Marco Island Writers Inc.

She resides on Marco Island with her husband, Tai.

You can find her books on her website at:
www.joannetailele.com or on Amazon.com.

The Artist

Kristine Taylor

Harrison's grandmother passed away during the night. He called the funeral home and they came to pick up the body. Her death was expected, but it still smarted. After the funeral director left, he leaned against the door, sobbing. He would miss her. She had lived with him for the past five years. She had such a positive attitude. He could talk with her about anything. Her advice was so reliable. At least now there was nothing holding him here in Mount Vernon, Iowa. He could move to downtown Chicago and pursue his dream of becoming a successful artist. He walked into his studio and began to paint a landscape with a church in it. It would take his mind off losing his grandmother. Since his parents died in a car accident five years ago, Grandma was one of the few relatives he had left.

Several days after the funeral, he drove to a restaurant to meet his friends Justin and Kevin. He arrived before them and took a seat in a booth near a window. A few minutes later, the men arrived. They gave their drink orders and began to peruse their menus. Just then two women walked by their table.

One of the women recognized Kevin. "Hey, Kevin!" the tall, blond woman said.

"Oh, hi, Lindsey," Kevin replied.

"This is my friend, Leigh."

"Hi, Leigh. This is Justin and Harrison. Listen, why don't you join us? We were just getting ready to order."

"Sure. That sounds like fun. Are you up for it, Leigh?"

"Awesome."

The women squeezed into the booth on either side.

"So, what's new with you, Harrison. How is your painting coming along?" Lindsay asked.

"Actually, I'm moving to Chicago in four weeks. I have some contacts downtown for several art shows."

"Oh, man. Well, you'll be missed."

"I'll be back to visit often."

"That's good."

Harrison couldn't take his eye off Leigh, staring as she picked up one of the menus. Her red hair cascaded down her back and her green eyes matched the green of her blouse. His fiancée had broken up with him several months earlier, so he was not on the market. His vow was to never get entangled with another woman as long as he lived. The heartache would destroy him. Leigh caught him staring at her. She was blushing as she ordered the lobster ravioli.

"Leigh works part time as an art critic for the Iowa City Tribune. She could do a piece on you, Harrison," Lindsey said.

"You are, really?" Harrison asked.

"Yes, I would love to do an article on you. What mediums do you use?"

"Watercolors and acrylics. I paint landscapes and abstracts. I'll be in several shows in Chicago this fall."

"Excellent," Leigh replied as she took in his dark brown hair slicked back with gel and brown eyes with gold flecks in them. His chiseled features made her heart beat a little faster. She couldn't remember meeting a more handsome man. They arranged to meet at his studio the next Saturday.

When Leigh arrived Saturday, Harrison took her jacket and hung it in hall closet. "Can I offer you something to drink?" he asked.

"Decaf if you have it."

"Sure, I just brewed some. Come into the kitchen." He poured two mugs of coffee. "My studio is back this way." He led her up a short flight of steps, along the hallway and turned left into a small room.

She gasped as she took in his paintings. There were ten landscapes with mountains, waterfalls, pine trees, churches, and rustic cabins. The room also held several abstracts with metallic colors, pastels, and bright colors.

"These paintings are exquisite. I am so glad you are willing to do this interview," Leigh said.

"Thank you. I'm sure a complimentary review from you will do wonders for my sales."

"So why are you moving to Chicago?"

"I was staying here to care for my grandmother. She died. I like the fast pace and action of the big city. I think there are more opportunities for an artist."

"But Mount Vernon is your hometown?"

"Sure is. I like it here, don't get me wrong. But the big city is where I belong."

"I would never leave this town. It's in my blood. I have so many friends here. I can't imagine starting over somewhere completely new," she said.

He savored the pleasant scent of her flowery perfume as she looked around in the room.

"Let's start the interview," she said, getting her tape recorder from her purse. "Where do you find inspiration for your paintings?"

"I travel a lot and work from photos or outside in nature."

"Why do you work in watercolors and acrylics?"

"Acrylics dry fast and watercolors are difficult but they have a special quality like no other medium. You can use them for foggy landscapes."

"How long have you been painting?"

"I started when I was in middle school. I've probably been painting for fifteen years."

"What is your price range for these paintings?"

"Anywhere from $200 to $1000. The prices are marked on the back here."

Harrison pointed out the price tags on the backs of his paintings.

Leigh finished the interview and made a date with him to review the article before it was published.

"I really enjoyed getting to know you," Leigh said as she gathered up her things. "So, I'll see you next week?"

"Excellent."

On Wednesday Leigh came to Harrison's door again and rang the doorbell.

"Hey," Harrison said as she walked in. "We can talk at the kitchen table." They walked through the living room and into the kitchen.

"Do you want coffee again?" Harrison asked.

"Sure, that would be great."

She took a copy of her article from her briefcase and smiled her approval as she caught a whiff of his spicy cologne.

"I'll let you read this first and see what you think."

He picked up the article and began to read.

"Wow, this is awesome! I like your writing. Thank you for doing this. You know, I was going to ask you something. I was wondering if you wanted to go out for dinner sometime. I am kind of on the rebound now, but I think we have a lot in common."

"Oh, Harrison, I really can't at this point. My fiancé left me at the altar and I've kind of sworn off men."

"My girlfriend left me, too, so I can relate. Can't we just have dinner once? I promise I'll be a gentleman."

"Well, okay. I guess one dinner can't hurt," Leigh said.

Friday evening, Leigh arrived at the Watermark Grille. She saw Harrison right away.

"Hi!" she said as she sat down in the booth. She wore a green and gold floral dress with black high heels. Her red hair had large curls.

"So, have you started packing for your move?"

"Yes, I've been donating a ton of stuff to Goodwill. I have a lot of books, but I'll take most of them with me."

"I have a lot of books too."

"What kinds of books do you read?"

"Mainly Christian fiction, romance, women's fiction, and biography."

"Oh, that sounds interesting."

"It is."

"So, what do you do for a day job?" Harrison asked.

"I'm a nurse at Iowa City Hospitals and Clinics. I work in the maternity ward. I help deliver babies."

"Wow! Are you an R.N. or an LPN?"

"I'm an R.N. Do you paint full time?"

"No. I teach at the Mount Vernon Center for the Arts, and I paint in my free time."

"Do you like teaching?"

"Yes. The students are very motivated, and I like painting examples for my classes."

"Do you have siblings?" Leigh asked.

"Yes, I have a brother and sister. They both live in Lake Geneva, Wisconsin. My brother lives in a five-bedroom home on the lake and my sister just built a home on the outskirts of town. It makes it convenient to visit them. They always have extra room and they live fifteen minutes apart. My brother is in finance and my sister is a veterinarian."

"Hmm. Sounds like a successful family."

"Where's your family?" Harrison asked.

"My parents live in Iowa City. They are retired. My siblings live in the suburbs of Chicago. One brother is an EMT and the other is the president of an Internet company. One sister is a writer and the other is a homemaker. What do you do for fun?" Leigh asked.

"I'm into windsurfing. I also like to read, especially when I want to relax. I like Steven James, Tom Clancy, John Grisham, and Stephen King."

Over coffee, they talked and talked, relaxed, comfortable in one another's company when a silence developed.

"I was wondering if you would like to watch me windsurf sometime. We could go to Black Hawk Lake when the wind is up."

"Sounds like fun. Call me," Leigh said.

Outside the restaurant, Harrison followed Leigh to her car. He put his fingers under her chin and tilted her face up for a kiss. It was soft and tender and she didn't want to drive away. Instead, she wanted that moment to last forever.

Harrison called Leigh the next evening after work. "Hey. I was wondering if you would like to go to Black Hawk Lake on Saturday. The wind is supposed to be 10-15 mph. It will be perfect for windsurfing."

"Sure. Should we meet there at noon?"

"Perfect."

Leigh arrived at Black Hawk Lake promptly at noon. She saw Harrison sitting in his car with the air conditioning running full blast. He jumped out of his car when he saw her and gave her a warm hug before getting his windsurfing equipment from his trunk. Leigh carried a small cooler with their picnic lunch in it and together they walked to the lake.

"How did you get into windsurfing?" Leigh asked.

"My dad was into sailboat racing for most of my life. Then a friend of mine introduced me to windsurfing. It's really fun jumping waves."

Soon they were at the edge of the lake. Harrison assembled his windsurfing equipment and walked with it into the crashing waves. He hopped onto his board and began to skim over the waves.

Leigh spread a towel at the lake's edge and settled down with a book by her side. *What am I doing with this guy? He's going to be leaving for Chicago in a few weeks. I don't want to get my heart broken again.* Harrison was out pretty far now. The wind was the perfect speed. She waved to him, as he sailed back in toward her. Soon the wind began to diminish, and Harrison surfed into the shoreline. He jumped off his board and walked up to where Leigh was sitting.

"That was awesome!" Leigh said. "You are so good at that."

"Thanks. It is so fun." He set his equipment down next to Leigh and sat down next to her.

"May I have a sandwich?"

"Sure. I've got ham and Swiss, egg salad, Pringles and lemonade."

"Cool. Ham and Swiss sounds good." Harrison began to eat. "Mmm. This is delicious." *What am I doing with this beautiful woman when I am leaving in several weeks?* Harrison thought. *I've had my heart broken once…I don't want it to happen again.*

"Isn't it a beautiful day?" Harrison said.

"Sunny and warm. No sign of rain."

"Too bad the wind died."

"Yeah. We'll have to continue it another day."

Harrison and Leigh finished eating and then they walked back to the parking lot. He put his equipment in his trunk and turned to Leigh.

"I had fun today. We should get together again soon. Do you like movies?"

"Yes, I do. Let me guess. You like action movies."

"And you like dramas or romantic comedies? We can see whatever you want."

"I saw the previews of a movie called the Red, Red Rose. It's a romance. I love romances."

"Ugh! I guess I can suffer through that."

"You better watch out…you might like it."

"Should I pick you up Friday at 6:30 p.m.?" Harrison asked.

"Sure. I'll see you then." Harrison leaned down to kiss her goodbye. She responded enthusiastically and after a minute he came up for air.

"So, I'll see you later?" Leigh said breathlessly.

"I'm looking forward to it."

Leigh waited by her front window for Harrison to arrive for their movie date. She was still a little nervous about seeing Harrison even though she had been dating him for a couple weeks. She so wanted to please him. She saw him pull into the parking lot and walked out to his car.

"Hey," Harrison said after he got out of his car to open her door.

Harrison felt his heart racing as he took her hand. He had never felt such a strong attraction before. She was everything he wanted in a woman. She was beautiful, smart, funny, and interesting. He was actually rethinking his move to Chicago. He couldn't believe a woman could affect him this way. They walked up to the ticket booth and Harrison paid for both tickets. They walked into the theater and took their seats in the middle of the room. Harrison took her hand in his. The movie turned out to be better than he expected and he found it to be a riveting story. Half way through, Harrison put his arm around Leigh. She felt safe and warm in his embrace. She wondered if there was any way he would cancel his move to Chicago to be with her. Maybe he would invite her to come with him. She wouldn't do that. She couldn't. After the movie ended, they drove to a Pete's Pizza restaurant, a food they had discovered they both liked. They were seated right away.

"Would you like to share a veggie pizza?" Leigh asked.

"Sounds good. Although I'm kind of a carnivore."

"We could compromise. Let's order sausage and veggies."

"Even better."

"I really enjoyed that movie," Leigh said.

"Yeah, wasn't it powerful?"

"Next time you get to choose the movie."

"Awesome. Action movies are very entertaining."

"I like them. I just like dramas and comedies better."

"Fair enough. What did you like about the movie?"

"I liked the happy ending and the conflict seemed natural and not contrived."

"I thought the couple had incredible chemistry. I don't know how they pulled that off."

"The casting department must have been excellent."

"Yeah, no doubt."

The server came around to take their order.

"We'll have a sausage and veggie pan pizza with iced coffee and lemonade."

The server took their menus and left.

"So, who are your favorite authors?" asked Harrison

"I like Karen Kingsbury, Brandilyn Collins, Dee Henderson, Terri Blackstock, and Kristin Billerbeck. All Christian authors, I know."

"If that's who you like, I have no problem with it."

"Are you a Christian?"

"I believe in God, but I'm not a regular church-goer."

"I'm a devout cradle Catholic."

"Good for you. I totally respect that."

Leigh digested Harrison's words and deduced he was not a controlling man. She liked that.

"How is your painting going?"

"I think your article did wonders for my sales. All seven of my paintings at a Mount Vernon gallery sold out in the first week of this month. I have to submit ten more within the next three days so needless to say, I've been busy."

"That's great! I'm glad I could help you with that."

Leigh's joy at being able to help him dissolved a little as a tinge of sadness appeared, thinking of him leaving town soon. "Who is going to promote you when you move to Chicago?"

"I'm actually thinking of staying here in Mount Vernon. You have mesmerized me. I can't imagine my life without you."

"That is exactly what I wanted to hear."

THE END

195

About the Author

Kristine Taylor

Born in Beloit, Wisconsin, Kristine Taylor was raised in north central Illinois. She was an avid reader from an early age. The highlight of her youth was participating in equestrian events as part of the United States Pony Clubs. Her college years were spent at the University of Iowa in Iowa City, Iowa, where she was an English major. Taylor is a member of several writing organizations. She is currently writing an inspirational romance novel. Her short stories and poems have been published in several anthologies. Her hobbies are scrapbooking, photography, playing the piano, and painting. Marco Island, Florida has been her home for the past 18 years.

THE MISSING TREE

Linda Walker

The Advent season was approaching. The worship committee of the United Methodist Church was making their plans for the festive season. The Chrismon tree had to be put up and decorated. The Nativity scene had to be brought from the closet and set up. Which meant someone had to retrieve the table used for its placement. The banners would have to come out of storage and be ironed prior to being hung on the sanctuary walls. Garlands of greenery would be placed around the windows and the Advent wreath would have to be prepared and new candles purchased. Lots to do and, as usual, too few volunteers to go around.

As chairwoman of the committee, Carol, with her sister Eileen as co-chairwoman, had gathered a small group of volunteers in the meeting room to make their plans.

Having two sisters on a committee could result in one of two scenarios. In one, they stand together on the plans they prepared prior to the meeting. In the other, they each have their differing ideas and each has her backers on the committee which results in sisterly quibbling. Either way no one else has a chance of having an idea accepted.

Having decided on the way to the church that each sister should have her half of the committee in charge of specific portions of the decorating, the sisters began to squabble.

Carol, hating ironing, being short and without a husband to commandeer to hang the banners, wanted Eileen's group to handle the banners. She also wanted Eileen's group to take care of the hanging of the garlands for two of those same reasons. Carol thought arranging the Nativity scene and preparing the Advent wreath should be the responsibility of her group of volunteers.

Since the Chrismon tree was very large, both groups would have to work on it. Of course, Eileen's husband being tall and strong could handle getting the tree out of storage and setting it up. He would also come in handy in placing the lights on the Chrismon tree and decorating it where the ladies couldn't reach. Eileen wasn't sure her husband, Joe, would be available on the Friday and Saturday before the first Sunday of Advent. Did any of the other volunteers have a husband to help out?

When all the squabbling was over, the assignments were set in stone just as Carol had wanted. She being the older sister and pulling rank in both sisterhood and as committee chairwoman made the decision.

Now each group had to determine where last year's committee had stored everything and retrieve it all. The closet at the back of the narthex was checked out, as was the storage area in the fellowship hall. As each box of items was discovered they were dragged into the meeting room and divided between the two groups. Each group subdivided the portions of their respective assignments according to Carol and Eileen's directions. Everything was accounted for except the Chrismon tree and its decorations. It was not in the narthex closet or the fellowship hall storage area. Where could that tree be?

Since it was so big maybe someone had taken it home to store in their garage. Questions would have to be asked of last year's committee members. Who was on the committee last year was the first question to ask. Of course, not all former committee members were back for the season. Some may even have died over the past year. Who had time to call everyone? Assignments were made and calls placed. No one seemed to remember what had been done with the tree. No one seemed to have it in their possession. Where was that tree?

The first Sunday of Advent came. The church looked splendid. The banners brightened the walls, greenery ran along all the windows and the Nativity scene was in its place next to the choir loft. The Advent wreath was in place next to the pulpit with all new candles ready for the lighting ceremony. Poinsettias lined the altar rail, sat before the communion table and filled a larger than usual area of the altar platform. Including the space where the Chrismon tree formerly stood. Many parishioners did not even notice the missing tree with all those poinsettias. Those that did wondered why there was no tree but for the most part nothing was said about the missing tree. The worship committee gratefully accepted the compliments on the beauty of the Christmas decorations with a sigh of relief.

Prior to Christmas the church choir always hosted a lovely Christmas party at the home of one of the choir members. As only a few had homes large enough to hold the party for all who wanted to come, it had become a tradition that one hospitable member with a large home and a wife who loved to decorate held the party at their home. The hostess spent much time decorating the house with her Santa collection and multiple Christmas trees, at least one tree per room. Although some rooms had more, and, of course, there were the trees on the lanai by the pool. All the choir and church members who attended brought food to share and a wonderful time of fellowship was enjoyed by all.

Carol arrived at the party bearing her contribution to the Christmas goodies.

As she wandered through the house admiring the decorations, she asked her hostess, "Just how many Santas are in that display on the big armoire?"

"Oh, just 250," she replied.

"She has another 250," her husband added. "She displays the others on alternate years since they won't all fit up there at once. Have you seen her latest addition to the Christmas trees? Come with us and we'll show it to you."

Carol followed them into the foyer. There it stood. It was a magnificent Chrismon tree.

"Where did you ever get that, it's beautiful?" Carol said.

"Oh, I bought it at the annual rummage sale at the church last spring," she said. "Isn't it just magnificent? Such a perfect Chrismon tree and the decorations came with it. I always wanted a Chrismon tree for my collection. It's every bit as beautiful as the one we always had at the church. I wonder whatever became of that tree? I don't remember seeing it this year."

"Yes, said Carol, I wonder whatever became of that tree?"

THE END

About the Author

Linda Walker

Linda Walker has been a member of Marco Island Writers for several years. She has learned much in helping to edit this anthology.

Mom-Mom Goes to Rehab

(Book One of the "Mom-Mom and Me" series)

James J. Waltz

Skylar was so excited, his hands were shaking. He was finally going to visit Mom-Mom. It felt like it had been forever since he had seen her. Actually, it had only been three weeks, but school finished two whole weeks ago, and this past week was so boring. His Mama and Daddy had told him when he finished first grade he would get to spend the beginning of summer with Mom-Mom. And they even said he might get to spend the first week there without his little sister, Olivia.

"Just Mom-Mom and me?" Skylar had asked Mama, with a hint of a smile and a little twinkle in his eye.

"We'll see," said Mama. "depending on how Mom-Mom is feeling."

Skylar didn't quite understand what Mama meant by that, since he knew he and Mom-Mom always laughed and had fun when it was just the two of them together. Maybe it had something to do with what Skylar heard his Daddy say to Mama that night a while ago, when they thought he was asleep in the back seat of the car.

"Your Mom seemed worn out tonight," Daddy had whispered on the ride home from Sunday dinner at Mom-Mom's.

"I know, she looked tired. Maybe because she did so much this weekend," Mama said.

"Just keep an eye on her, and make sure she goes to see her doctor if she needs to," Daddy replied, as he reached over to hold Mama's hand, which Skylar could see through his half-closed eyelids. *To the doctor?* thought Skylar, beginning to worry as he drifted off to sleep for real.

A few days later, he was on the back porch trying to color in his superhero book, but Olivia kept taking his crayons to scribble in her own book. Just when he was thinking about doing something else, Mama came running out of the house with Skylar's backpack in her hand.

"Get your stuff together, quick," she yelled. "Mom-Mom's at the hospital, so I'm going to drop you two off at Uncle Jimmy's on my way over there."

"But I want to go with you to see Mom-Mom," Skylar cried.

"Don't start," she snapped. Then Mama took a deep breath and leaned down to hold his face in her hands, while Olivia started crying. "Be Mama's good boy and help your sister get in the car, and I promise I will take you to see Mom-Mom soon, just not today," she said as she kissed his forehead.

Those few weeks had seemed so long and slow, but now today was the day Skylar was finally going to visit Mom-Mom. His Uncle Jimmy had tried to explain to him that Mom-Mom wasn't in the hospital anymore, she was someplace sort of like a hospital where people go to get better and stronger before they go home. But Uncle Jimmy was laughing so much when he kept repeating "Mom-Mom's in Rehab!"

So Skylar and Mama and Daddy and even Olivia had taken the long car ride to visit Mom-Mom. When they parked outside the big building with all the glass windows, he practically jumped out of the car. Mama kept pulling on the back of his T-shirt telling him he needed to slow down. Skylar continued bouncing up and down as they were waiting while Daddy told the lady at the front desk Mom-

Mom's name. After checking her computer, the lady looked up and said "Oh, she's actually in the gym right now for therapy, but they will probably let you stay in the back and watch while she finishes." She told Daddy how to get there, then they all started walking down the long hallway. Mama said it felt like a maze with all the turns they were taking, but then they saw the big room with all the people. Skylar and Olivia stared wide-eyed at the sight of all the balloons and balls being tossed in the air!

There were a lot of people sitting in a big circle, each of them holding onto the edge of a brightly colored parachute, moving their arms up and down to make the balls in the middle go up in the air. Olivia tried to get down out of Daddy's arms, while Mama and Skylar looked to find Mom-Mom. He broke into a run when he saw her, as Mom-Mom smiled with her arms wide open to capture him in a hug. He barely noticed the small clear tube wrapped on her face and nose until they stopped hugging.

"Oh, hon, I feel so much better now that I've had one of our special hugs," Mom-Mom said as she held onto Skylar's arms. Mama leaned in to kiss her, when the lady sitting next to Mom-Mom said "He's adorable."

Olivia finally squeezed her way in between them, and when she started pulling on that tube on Mom-Mom's face a man came over to them.

"Careful, sweetie, you don't want to pull on that," he said, as he introduced himself to Mama and Daddy. Skylar heard him say his name was Tony, and he was some kind of therapist working with Mom-Mom and all the other patients there. He said the tube gave Mom-Mom oxygen to help her breathe better. Skylar didn't quite understand why it was in a tube, since his teacher had said oxygen was everywhere in the air all around. But before he could ask about it, Tony asked if Skylar and Olivia wanted to help everyone play with the parachute some more.

"Can we, Mama? Can we?!" they asked excitedly.

"I guess so," said Mama. "But keep your indoor voices, and no running."

Tony and another therapist named Dawn explained to all the people in the circle that they had to raise their arms up really high to make the parachute go up in the air. When it went up it looked like a big tent, and Tony yelled for Skylar and Olivia to run under it to cross to the other side of the circle. They got to play under the parachute for a while, running and laughing and even throwing the balls with Tony and Dawn. Olivia kept giggling as Skylar grinned from ear to ear, with Mom-Mom smiling at them the whole time. When Dawn said it was time to take a break and rest, Mama gestured for them to come over to her.

"That looked like fun," she said. "But it's almost lunch time, so you need to calm down a little now."

Skylar and Olivia wanted to try to help push Mom-Mom in her wheelchair out of the gym, but it turned out to be easier to let Daddy do the pushing.

The rest of the day visiting with Mom-Mom went way too fast for Skylar. Before he knew it, Daddy was saying it was time to head home.

"No, not yet," Skylar started to say, but Mom-Mom quickly pulled him into a big hug, and he couldn't talk as his face pressed into her. He felt his throat get tight and his eyes start to water, but he knew he didn't want to cry, so he just kept his face pressed against Mom-Mom.

"You're such a good boy, I love you so much," Mom-Mom whispered in his ear as she rubbed her hand on the back of his head. Skylar stood next to her holding onto her arm as everyone else gave Mom-Mom a hug good-bye. Then he got to spend a few more moments hugging Mom-Mom again as Mama and Daddy were talking to some nurses out in the hallway.

He felt so happy he had that extra time there with Mom-Mom, because he could still smell her on his clothes on the ride home. Olivia was already asleep, and Sklyar was just about to drift off when he heard Mama ask Daddy "Are you sure you won't mind? It will only be for a week or two."

Daddy reached over to hold Mama's hand. "It will be fine. And I have a feeling the kids would love to have her stay with us for a while."

Skylar popped up between the front seats as far as his seat belt would let him, not a bit tired anymore. "What? When?" he asked.

"Hush, hush," Mama said. "Don't wake your sister."

She turned and reached out to touch his cheek, smiling as she told him, "Mom-Mom is going to come live with us for a little while now."

Skylar practically bounced up and down, and his hands started shaking again the way they always did when he got excited. Mama didn't even tell him to calm down this time, she just smiled and turned to Daddy saying, "He's not going to sleep tonight, I bet you."

Skylar didn't care if he slept or not. He just sat back in his seat and looked out the car window at all the night stars in the sky, thinking, *Mom-Mom's coming home!*

THE END

About the Author

James J. Waltz

James J. Waltz is a licensed Occupational Therapist who was born and raised in New Castle, Delaware. As a young adult James had aspirations of becoming a professional actor, eventually joining Actors Equity and Screen Actors Guild, and he still maintains membership in both unions, because you never know where life will take you. He went on to live in Baltimore, Maryland for over 20 years with his life partner David (now legal spouse), working as a home healthcare Occupational Therapist.

After a permanent move to Naples, Florida in 2015, James sought out other creative venues, and recently joined the Marco Island Writers group. He continues to work in home health, and hopes to combine his experience as a therapist with his creative side to produce a children's book series entitled *Mom-Mom and Me,* about a young boy and his family encountering various levels of healthcare with his aging grandmother. This story, *Mom-Mom Goes to Rehab,* is intended as book one of the series.

Goodnight World

Shirley Woolaway

It is seven years since it happened. I was so unprepared. But
then how can one prepare for the worst thing that can happen
to a parent. The day started differently than usual. My
husband, Tom, and I were in New York, staying not at our
Mayville cottage but at Hotel St. Elmo in the Chautauqua
Institution community. With us was our granddaughter,
Sarah, 10, taking her first sailing course.
Sarah and I had biked back from the sailing club and eaten
lunch. She was reading, Tom, napping. I checked my phone
for messages. How I'd like to stop that day right there and
erase the rest from my memory as Tom's dementia would
for him. Tomorrow morning on awakening, he'd have no
memory of this afternoon. I envied him then. That his brain
had not recoiled in shock as mine had. That his body hadn't
felt the destructive words punching, splitting, exploding
inside his gut. He'd have no idea that his world was
shattered. He'd have no tears to share with me, no
comforting words.
I retrieved the latest message. It was from our son, Jeff's
neighbor, whom we'd met once on a Colorado visit. It
seemed strange that she was calling me, someone that I
hardly knew. There was no preamble like, "Hello, this is
Beth whom you met last summer when you visited Jeff."
There was not even, "I have some bad news. You might want
to sit down." Instead, it was: "Mrs. Woolaway, this is Beth,
from Colorado. Your son died last night and the police

208

stopped here this morning to tell us. I needed to let you know."

How can I describe what happened then? I felt like I could hardly breathe, like I'd been shot. I know I screamed and cried, "No.no, it can't be. No, it isn't true." I think I dropped my phone and Sarah came running in. I think I went to Tom crying and put my arms around him. At some point, I wanted to call T.A. and Brad our sons, our other sons. I became aware of phone messages from them. I called Brad. "Mom, I know. I tried to reach you. We're on our way and we'll be there in two hours. T.A. is leaving too and we'll meet at the cottage."

My wounded brain tried to take that in. The cottage, but how could we meet at the cottage because we had guests there, a favor to a single mom. When I protested, Brad's response, "Mom, you'll have to tell them to leave," penetrated this time.

The cottage. Yes, the cottage. Earlier I'd had a report from my friend about how they were enjoying our home and the lake. A working mom with three jobs, she needed this break. I silently asked for help, for a solution. An idea came and after talking with an understanding St. Elmo Hotel manager, an exchange of places would solve this small problem.

My mind and body connected enough to clean out the refrigerator and take off soiled sheets. Soon Brad arrived with Karen, Sarah's parents. "Mom sit down, we have to talk. There is more to Jeff's story. So, I sat and I listened and my gut twisted and the sobs came. Have they stopped?

I couldn't write this earlier, but now seven years later I think about him and can see the words I'm writing. What could have made his story end differently? What did I miss? Someday I'll write that story, but not today. No, this day, I just want to focus on him, my son.

Even as a baby, Jeff was a charmer. Baptized at Trinity Church in Beaver, Pennsylvania, he seemed to enjoy being the center of attention, smiling and opening his arms wide to the congregation and their applause. He captured my heart too, after I had been ambivalent about his birth, with his brother T.A. just 14 months old when he arrived.

I pick up a picture of Jeff as a four-year-old dressed for the photographer in a blue plaid jacket with brass buttons and a white shirt. His expression is wistful, like he wants to be hugged. So, I hug his picture and cry. It was taken in 1964, the year his younger brother, Brad arrived. In another picture with his brothers taken a few years later, Jeff has a mischievous grin. He was "always full of it," as his Welsh grandmother, liked to say.

I think of the day when he ran away from home at the age of 9, his response to his dad's correction the night before for not helping with chores. Jeff was complaining and difficult at breakfast on that hot July morning actually saying he was going to run away from home. I didn't take him seriously, saying, "Sure, I'll help you pack." Busy with laundry and expecting him to be with his friends or brothers in the nearby woods, a phone call from a neighbor alerted me to his whereabouts. She thought she'd seen Jeff walking on the far side of our town over three miles from home. "Isn't he too young to be down there by himself?" After calling his dad who went out searching for him, I stayed by the phone praying for his safety. I remember our panic. Several hours later, when Jeff stopped at a stranger's home to request a glass of water, the good Samaritan called us. "This young boy with a sunburned face, is he your son?" His brothers and I left immediately following the given directions and found him ten miles from home on his way to his grandmother's house. Today I can smile remembering his determination, his awareness of the correct route and the relief we felt. In three more miles, he'd have been there.

Another memory comes of the time in eighth grade, when he asked his teachers what his grades would be when report cards came out. He presented the grades with all his teacher's signatures to his dad. With an improvement in all of them, he got the dirt bike he'd been angling for a week before report cards came out.

I remember, too, an older Jeff, after high school, graduation from college, working as a successful salesman in Boston. His dad and I, with T.A. and his wife Carolyn, took a ski vacation to visit Jeff, then working at Snow Mass, Colorado, a ski resort. He suggested a picnic lunch half way up the mountain. He'd bring the food and some of his work buddies. I picture us sitting around the picnic table in our ski parkas, the sun warm overhead. I can almost smell the chili, the burgers, and French fries. Jeff was in his element, food, friends, a party and love of the mountains. I knew we'd never get him back to Pennsylvania.

I last saw him in February, six months before he died, when he visited us at our Marco Island condo with his girl-friend, HaThi. There was talk of a possible marriage, even a child. I was hopeful.

But, before the visit he'd damaged a knee, the second one, cleaning snow off his roof at the top of a mountain. In the summer, he had a prostate cancer scare and shared his anxiety about getting Alzheimer's like his dad. The weekend before he died, he had a vasectomy and broke off the relationship with his much younger girlfriend. Another painkiller was added to his medicine chest. A year earlier, his doctor switched him from too many Tylenol (bad for your liver) to a narcotic. It worked better to dull the pain of his 50 year-old body, damaged by years of over-exuberant activity: skiing, boating, biking, hiking, and sports.

In Pennsylvania, my focus then was on downsizing, clearing out furniture and everything else at our home. It had sold quickly and the closing was in a month and a half. The plan was to move to our Marco Island condo to simplify life and eliminate traveling back and forth. Jeff couldn't come back just then, he said because of work which had been slim during the winter months. I was disappointed and a visit to Colorado seemed out of the question then with all my energy directed towards being ready for the closing date.

Tom could not help with the moving activities, did not feel the pressure of the closing, could not enter my world. He did not miss Jeff as I did when the family got together to claim household items they could use.

One month later we viewed Jeff, so still, so unnatural at a Colorado funeral home. With our family and HaThi, we received his neighbors and friends who shared our loss and gave us hugs. Tom was disoriented by the trip. But he seemed to grieve, to be sad or was it just me wanting him to share some of what I felt. Tom never spoke of Jeff after the memorial service and outlived his middle son by three and a half years.

Months after Jeff's death, I read about the high incidence of suicide in the Rocky Mountains. One explanation was that the higher elevation caused pain medication to be much more potent. This helped me understand, a little, how my son could do what he did. His note to his dad and me, his brothers, "I'm sorry, but I just can't handle the pain any more. I love you very much, Jeff."

As I write this, seven years to the day he wrote that note, I think about him. A picture from earlier Colorado visits to his condo comes to me: Jeff stepping out on his balcony before bed, finding peace in the brilliance of the stars against the dark sky and hearing him say, "Goodnight world." I'd like to imagine him doing that seven years ago and that those were his last words.

THE END

Recipe for peace

Shirley Woolaway

Ingredients:

Begin with: Men, women, teenagers, children from many
states and other countries

 Add: Speakers, citizens of the world who share their lives
to inform, challenge, and inspire to action

Throw in: leisure, time to mull & turn over new thoughts
and try them out

Add: Prosperity, enough so that leisure is possible for a
weekend, a week, a month or more

Mix in: Spiritual thinkers, Christian, Jewish, Muslim, others
who guide us away from darkness to light

Sprinkle in: Wide front porches, wicker chairs, rockers,
iced tea, ice cream, and words

Add: Gobs of color, yellow, purple, red, and spicy scents
from small gardens

Dribble in: Shades of blues from lake and sky

Pour in: Liquid when the gray skies open, only enough to
keep the mix intact

Add: Lots of green from tall oaks, maples, beeches,
whispering their songs to any who listen

Mix in: Lots of children playing Frisbee or Nerf ball, riding bikes, calling out to friends

Include: Music from a lone fiddler playing Celtic dances, from 65 musicians, one singer or 100

Add: Respect, lots of it, especially when his views are so strange

Mix in: Love for one another and most especially the other

Cream all this together, bake in the sunshine for one to nine weeks, and you'll have PEACE.

About the Author

Shirley Musgrave Woolaway

Shirley received a BA in Advertising from Pennsylvania State University after working as a journalist on both the newspaper and yearbook publications. Shirley wrote features for several newspapers after graduation and married her college beau, Tom Woolaway.

While raising three sons, she became active in community organizations, serving as a member of the Beaver Area School Board and as president of Women in Communications, Pittsburgh.

After working as an account exec for several ad agencies, Shirley operated her own boutique agency, Musgrave Woolaway Advertising for five years before switching careers. She earned an M Ed in Community Counseling from Duquesne University, Pittsburgh and worked as a therapist primarily for women in crisis.

While Shirley was a caregiver for her Alzheimer afflicted husband, she started a support group for those with dementia and their caregivers, first in Sewickley, PA and for the last seven years at St. Mark's Church, Marco Island where she is an active member.

Currently, she writes family stories and a column on dementia for the Coastal Breeze newspaper. Shirley is a member of the Marco Island Writers group. She continues to take writing classes, primarily at Chautauqua Institution in New York during their nine-week summer sessions. She wrote the *Recipe for Peace* in a rocking chair on St. Elmo Hotel's porch, while observing activities in the central square.

Poets' Corner

"Why Marco Island?"

Why not, Marco?

Why not hide out here on this
    Gulf's stretched shore all winter long
        veiled from the
            fierce falling
                snows railing above us?

Why not be thankful for
    plots of potential salsa,
        gourmet greeneries and
            orchard trees squeezed
                just down the lane?

Why not celebrate your holidays
    among inflamed poinsettias
        dancing on patios
            rather than those ugly plastic wreaths
                stuck in frost plastered windows.

Why not welcome the New Year in with
    warmth winning dog days
        instead of stuck in a storm
            with snow trapped
                wheels spinning around?

Why not feel sweltering beams
    from your lordly lounge chair
        resting in a sandy dune
            rather than see shadows
                in snowbanks at dawn?

Why not share with your
        bikini clad love
                a sugared
                        valentine on a
                                horizon of white fine?

Why not bless an Easter
        eggy sunrise under
                gem-colored heavens and
                        peaceful waving palms that
                                chant in the air?

Why not contemplate that
        sailor's delight ...
                a red sky at night... with a
                        limey flash of hope in
                                a drunken sunset?

Why not Marco?

                                S. Clay

                                10/1/17

About the Author

Sara Clay

Sara has been a member of Marco Island Writers Group for three years. and is the founder of Poets Corner sub-group.

She lives in Boston and winters on Marco.

Sara wrote her poem "Why Marco Island?"in response to an article in the Marco Newspaper about a contest entitled "Why Winter on Marco Island?"

Having written, sung, danced and lived poetry all her life, the author describes poetry as "her private love."

ARE ALL CATS GREY IN THE DARK?

Nick Kalvin MD

At cocktails, gossip made rounds to me:
A scandal in local gynecology.
"Homely wench irate when Doc broke free!
Even wrote to the Board." The news floored me.

What lured him? Nothing partiers could see.
(Frenchmen say, it's not what's twixt les knees,
Makes a girl unique or sweet. *"Mais, oui.*
"Pendant la nuit, tous les chats sont gris."
But, yes. During the night, all cats are grey).

Somehow, this puss oozed desirability,
Dazed, lured him into dumb duplicity.
Guys want looks, a brain, for their checkout cart,
Plus, love beaming from a female heart.

I quizzed men bar-hopping for a weekend tart.
Wrote quotes, penned check-marks on my chart.
Each said, "Indeed smiles, curves grab my heart."
(No mention as to cute atypia of the nether part).

As a doc, I know to be an OB is not easy:
Long hours, tough births, at least one nightly emergency,
Douches, discharge, BC pills, periods, pregnancy,
VD, cramps, yeast and warts, each day, to see.
A list which might make horny Don Juan queasy.

In that stirrup-view, as his examinee,
Did Plain-Jane show him rare, exotic scenery?
Folks said, "She can't converse, flirt gracefully,
Lacks social skills, grades zero as to virtuosity."

Poor colleague! Why such reckless urgency?
Brain rot, hormones, voodoo, mid-life insanity?
No one could explain this weird affair to me!
I put his clean record, alms, morals in my testimony.

THE POUNDING SEA, THE STORM AND ME

Out there, storm clouds kissing the Sea,
    Their soft thundering beckons me.
That same old salt in all my veins,
    Contained in foam of crashing waves.

So, blood kin, we must surely be,
    Creature, salty mist, pounding sea,
Crossing arcs during our brief spans,
    Here on Southwest Florida sands.

Big Bang remnants persist in us,
    Make up dear Mother Earth's warm crust.
All things, and I, briefly exist
    Mingled here in warm twilight mist.

This sea, this sea, this pounding sea,
    Calls, reminds, connects with me...
Same brine in red blood and white froth,
    Brothers by same Great Power wrought.

Co-existing wonders that I see,
    Cooled star dust kin, Your sea and me.
Sweet, dear life, love and hope each brings,
    Midst soft misty gusts whisperings.

Beauty, blessed things we surely be,
    That lovely pounding sea and me.
This gifted day on Naples' shore,
    Thankfulness stirs in my core,

Tearfully joining flesh and soul
    To throbbing, foaming swells that roll,
Exhilarating in late sun,
    While our fleeting spans do run.

Sharp awareness, and what I see
    Join me to You, your pounding sea.

Nick Kalvin, M.D.
Submitted to Florida Weekly from picture prompt, August 14, 2012

BARBIE AND MAURICE WERE RIGHT
(BARBIE'S ANNIVERSARY)

Nick Kalvin M.D.

"Math is hard," chirped the newest, cutest Barbie Doll.
Feminists gagged, like cats, choking on a large fur ball,
Yowled, "Differences are not based on genes at all."
Say, "Boys and girls are not the same," will start a brawl.
Yet, schools find: Boys best at math and science after all.

Girls in art, music, spelling. When young, more tall,
Cleaner, more alert, prepared, when teachers call.
In labs, male toddlers climb fences. Little girls sit, or start
to bawl.
At home, Sis helps Mom. Bro runs, heeds adventure's call

Boys love outdoors, sports. Girls color, play house, hug a
doll.
Girls jump rope, dress-up, rhyme. Boys dirty, loud, quite
physical,
Play war, wrestle, ruin clothes. Girls' games and teas, so
pastoral.
Then, years after, TIME MAGAZINE made an astounding
claim:

"Research proves, boys and girls are NOT the same!
(But, variance between them is no cause for shame.
Each has duds and grand outliers, who will excel, win
acclaim).
Vive la différence," crooned a Frenchman of movie fame,
"Without little girls, what would little boys do?" his refrain.

222

THAT BIKE OUT THERE ON OUR LAWN

Nick Kalvin, M.D. ©

It was left right here, her twisted bike upon our grass.
But, gone is our news girl, a bright and cheerful lass,
Pretty little scholar, crossing guard for her class.
For her poor parents, heartache will never pass.
Damned daylight savings, forced her out into the dark,
Peddling morning papers, from her home up to the park.
Wife and I heard tires screech. Dogs began to bark.
Medics shook their heads. Cop measured tire marks.
At last, the SOB was nabbed. Illegal. Uninsured.
Had two DUIs, the neighbor later heard.
Driver's clunker: bad brakes, one head-light out. He's a jail
bird.
To be deported again. It's said, this time's the third.
Clever, cute paper girl made page one, the day she was
interred.

BRAHMAN'S LOVING SON

Nick Kalvin MD.

The place was India. September 8, 1910, the date,
Young Prince roamed a jungle, in his vast family estate,
Happy, unaware what tiny things can change one's fate.
Came upon a crawling creature, known as the Krait.

It was pretty, dew-bejeweled, out looking for a mate.
This lad, quite curious, (by far, his best genetic trait),
Watched the small snake, as morning hours turned late.
He had a net, carried on a strap, his small bamboo crate.

Last night, told Dad, "One day, Father, a grand zoo I'll
create."
He picked up the snake. It seemed to be in a placid state.
Being put in the crate turned snake's good mood acetate,
It bit his thumb. Yes, tiny fangs, but classed as cannulate.

"Such a tiny bite," Prince mused. But, felt things deteriorate:
Mouth grew numb. Trouble breathing would escalate:
"Best get home," he said. Got double vision, then a dizzy
state.
Sat to rest. Legs got weak. Sensed wakefulness dissipate.

Rajah's aide, found Prince, limp, in what seemed a resting
state.
When they looked in his shoulder-carry bamboo crate
Snake crawled out. Aide shouted, drew his sword, quite irate.
Rajah stayed his man's arm. "Prince loved all Brahman did
create."

Rajah and Rani that wild tract of land did soon dedicate.
Within it, built an immense Royal zoo meant to educate
Their nation's young, like their son and his schoolmates.
At the gate, stands bronze Prince. Folk read on his gilded base
plate,
"Welcome to this best of zoos, which I paid so dearly to
create."

ETERNAL MEMORY

Nick Kalvin MD ©

I got here early, after dawn,
To this peaceful, lush green lawn.
Reflecting, back through time,
Scenes and people pass in mind
As I rest under sympathetic trees,
A yellowed album on my knees.

View sweet memories made with you,
Some quite old, but, still seem new.
I've heard, "Undone deeds, words unsaid,
Cause most tears when someone's dead."
You taught me early, how life is grand,
But, much too short for reprimand.

Age confirms your words were true,
Now, I shed tears of thanks for you,
Who endured my worse teen phases,
Then, gently spoke your love in phrases.
It's Time to leave again. So, sad,
Time to bury a pipe for you, Dad,

A red rose, like you favored, Mom.
Soon, I'll go back to where I'm from,
To rendezvous at some distant scene.
What a dazzling day this has been,
Sun rays bleach, and my sins estrepe.
I sense them go. No more need to weep.

FADED PHOTO ON MY WALL

Nick Kalvin MD ©

Each day, I blow a kiss to your photo,
Above my dresser, then go on my way.
But, that poor picture, so long up on the wall,
Has yellowed some. The colors fade away.
Happy people, birds, waves, beach, golden sun,
All seem to dim, with the passing years,
You two, first son, Tom, me in uniform.
If, I stare too long, my eyes blur with tears.
We can't go back, lovely Mom, dearest Dad,
The blind/mute, trudge along, use up each day.
So please, tell me, how is it out there, where,
Loved ones stay and never fade away?

I wrote *Just an Orange Tree* a long time ago, during the Egypt-Israel war, after reading about a real incident in a news story. Several months later, I was at the Utah Society of Ophthalmology meeting in SW Utah. We had a motivational speaker, who said doctors kept too much suppressed emotion, fear, regret and frustration within. He urged us to begin each day with physical activity, like biking or running, even if we had to get up and out early, save time for reflection and rest . . . during each day . . . before surgery and after, even, if for a minute or two. He asked us each to share something emotional. Something, or some person, or event which touched us inside, and which illustrated how precious each moment is.

I told about being affected by this orange tree and described my poem. As I talked, tears came to my eyes, and to several others. I had to pause during the telling.

The meeting was in Cedar City, Utah, a lovely college town, which presented a summer series of Shakespeare plays on campus.

About a year or two later, that relatively young, same program chairman-motivational speaker collapsed, and died, one early morning, as he was tying up his running shoes, next to his Jeep, on a path in the mountains near where the meeting took place. I wrote to his widow about that surgical seminar and the sharing and how great a human being, doctor and man her spouse seemed to us who attended. I hoped his last view was a beautiful sunrise.

Interestingly enough, Israeli commanders in the Egypt-Israeli War found, in satellite photos, ancient trading trails from Biblical times, crossing NE Egypt. They used these trails to hide while travelling, and gain advantage to launch unexpected attacks on the Egyptian forces.

Nick Kalvin

JUST AN ORANGE TREE

Nick Kalvin MD ©

It was named, one-more "last" Arab-Israeli war.
In a cold, bomb-cratered orchard near the shore,
Squad stained with Cordite, dirt, sweat and gore,
Set out a guard, then, with all muscles stiff and sore,

Sat close, traded stale rations, all they had left to eat,
One chopped down a nearby tree, began a fire for some
heat,
At least, shot-up tractor tires made each man a seat,
A lost goat wandered near, became cuts of roasting meat.

When at last relieved, the first sentry came by.
He sat. Fire flickered, mirrored in his unpatched eye.
From it tears came forth and he began to cry.
Concerned, the officer asked him, "Private, why?"

Jacob, father, farmer, dreamer, an elder son,
He sobbed, "Please, look, Sir, at what we've done!
Killed and burned this orange tree, the surviving one!
I smelled its blossoms. Why, did not someone?

Poor, poor tree! It gave men such sweet food and drink.
Took so many years to grow. How low we creatures sink!
And, just for a brief bit of heat, don't you think?
From Eve's garden, it now turns to charcoal as I blink!"

Fearful, so far from home, safety, friends and kin,
Those grizzled, wounded, worn-out fighters cried with him.
War squandered Eden's gift and marked up one more sin,
Each man ached, shed tears as the sun died and dark crept
in.

228

FROM HERE TO ETERNITY
A LOVE AFFAIR

Nick Kalvin, MD ©

Day and night, she remains alluringly supine, that seductive
beach.
Sugary mounds, tempt timid wavelets up to lap at her and
reach
Around her curves from Cape Horn and Good Hope to
Galveston
Pretty Beach looks past those little boys. High tide is much
more fun.

Moon-struck, the ocean throbs and swells with mounting
anticipation,
To rise, then fall upon her, as it has, since the earth's
creation.
Twice a day, Beach awaits, absorbs swollen Ocean's urgent
pounding.
Briny tons assault and probe the Beach with thuds
resounding.

Ocean's turgid waves must recede, but clutch vainly at the
beach,
After plunging inland, as far as successive thrusts can
reach.
Spent, grand waves deflate with a hissing, foaming,
bubbling swish,
To leave, in Beach pools and crevices, more loads of little
fish.

BREATHING LOVE

Nick Kalvin MD

This vast mysterious universe is but one,
From onset 'til our time will be over, done.
Once, rays burst from a spot too small to see,
Yet, from emanations, all things condensed to be.

Within God's eternal time, our puny clocks exist.
Our eras, eons, less than seconds persist.
Because we came late in a Sacred Dream,
On this plush, protective planet set in solar scheme.

Our sun's role: Be the forge, then shrink and end.
All souls, back to somewhere will be sent.
But, the Holy Force will stay on to reign,
Make new time, new beings, new worlds, again.

We gaze at distant, lovely, sister stars,
From moist, green Earth, beyond dead, arid Mars.
Each breath brings His love into every breast,
Reminds us just how much we're blessed.

A sentient creature somehow become aware,
Mostly, dawn and sunset, there's a force out there.
It acts, eats, fears, loves, struggles to stay alive.
Born with a subconscious urge to survive.

With the gift of mind, Humans seek to imitate.
We reproduce, invent. In varied arts we create,
Ape our Maker, each in his or her own way.
Cave walls. Now, stone, paper, canvas, sound, baked clay.

Please, daily pause, inhale deep, and look around.
Planets like ours, we now know, are rarely found.
Greet each dawn and breath as more Divine gifts to us.
For, outside waits space, dark, cold and cavernous.

MIDNIGHT ANGEL

Nick Kalvin, M.D. ©

A Quiet night, on tenth floor,
A nurse's desk behind glass door,
Green-glow screens keeping score,
Dim hall floor lights, nothing more.
As white, crepe-soled shoes moved by,
So soft of tread, so slow and sly.
His gloved hand, last door knob tried.
Then, The Angel slipped inside.
Just too damned cruel, he thought,
For such brief and hard time bought,
When evil blood disease was caught
By this poor, dear, lovely tot.
He caressed her tiny feet,
Her wasted limbs beneath the sheet.
And her pretty face so sweet,
Whose loving gaze, his own did meet.
No more screams with marrow sticks,
No sore-veined, digging, needle pricks,
No more emetic, toxic mix,
No massive bruises like steel-toed kicks.
From a white coat pocket's deep,
He took a vial of Elysian sleep.
Pains and fears would soon estrepe,
Take her up, where souls never weep.
His two hands, steady, this time,
Pushed it into her IV line.
Honey colored drops, in a short time,
Would block the useless, painful kind.
Her pale lids fluttered, squeezed,
Cracked lips, with a last smile, creased.
She looked rested, peaceful, pleased,
Her chest's motion slowed, then ceased.
On the quiet elevator, going down,

231

Tears dripping. His sniffles the only sound,
At floor five, caused a student nurse to frown,
And blink dewy, doe-like eyes, soft brown.
She asked, "Did you lose someone dear?"
"Yes," his head down, throat not quite clear,
"At least, for now, nothing more to fear.
Nurse, it's been one Hellish year."

PATIENTS PAST, MOTORCYCLE VALKYRIE, 1959

Nick Kalvin, MD ©

She'd been unique. A lovely, amazing Amazon,
　　Then, one of special patients I'd come upon.
I pictured her in wind and sun, a biker Valkyrie,
　　Red hair streaming, leather clad, riding happily.
Her skin soft and creamy. Lustrous sapphire eyes.
　　Her old life style was hard for me to surmise,
Leashed by tie, white coat, grades, rigid med-school mode,
　　As she was out, free, roaring down some endless road.

But, a wreck and injuries moved her to this braked, rehab bed
　　Where we met. PT fellow and half-dead thoroughbred.
Her only crash, a bad one, ended a carefree, nomadic way,
　　Then put her into a wheel chair, where she'd stay.

I rolled up to her, with PT's newest electromyogram.
　　Would leg cells twitch, answer brain strip telegram?
Issue micro hints of hope, or just confirm a bad prognosis?
　　She watched my face. Upon it, read her own diagnosis.

I gently asked, "So sorry, Miss. Do you have a question?"
　　"I trust you, Doc. One I've been dying to mention.
Will feelings come back here?" pointed at her groin,
　　"By chance, can nerves down there somehow rejoin?"

I shook my head. Tears streamed from those goddess eyes.
　　I took her hand, "Miss, that's all gone. But, please realize,
You can still get pregnant. Female workings are still okay.
　　Numbness, paralysis below the waist? Both will stay."

I flipped switches, rolled wires, wiped the steel probe,
　　Rearranged her blue, terry-cloth, PT bathrobe.
She touched my sleeve, said "Doc, can you sit for a while?"
　　When I nodded, she raised her chin. Even tried to smile.

233

THE EDGE

Nick Kalvin MD

LIS	OOBE
I hear your steps	Strange sight below
Smell you, feel you	My white face
Miss you	Confusion, red
You read aloud	Dripping to the floor
Ask each day	Beeping noises
Am I still inside	Frying sounds and cuss words
Hug me, Kiss me	Wispy smoke curls up
You cry at times	A guy in green
Wipe your salty tears	Brings bags of blood
From my lips	Damn cyst for years oozed pus
When you leave	One messy pain in the ass
I draw back in, for hours replay	"We'll scrape it out
A silent slide-lantern show	Let it heal
Decades of you and me	An easy fix…"
Then, a long video	All goes black again
Living and the dead	I wake up
Family, friends, colleagues	You lean on the cart
In slow parade	Look down to say
They smile and wave	"There was a problem
Dissolve when	We handled it"
My strength ebbs	I nod "I know!"
Once more you come	Your eyes get wide
Wipe both our tears	I tell what I saw
Hold, kiss my face	Smelled, felt and heard
I'm weary of	Why my chest's so sore
Consultants' gab	This time it's
Pricking, pinching, poking	Your turn to
Feel each pain Marie	Fade to pale
But can't respond	Your chin and neck
Think it's time to go	White and wet with sweat
Back where I'm from	Reflect blueness
But oh my sweet	Of your scrubs
What I would do	You take my hand

234

If I could
One more time with you

I squeeze back

LIS: Locked-in syndrome, pseudo
coma

OOBE:Out-of-body experience

WHERE, IN WHAT, IS ALL THERE IS?

Nick Kalvin MD

In what huge amphora does all
Which has been, and will be, exist?
Made from naught, flashed from a tiny point
Fourteen billion years ago, we're told,
A bursting, hollowing sphere cluster racing to cold
Bleak emptiness. While in flight provides
A fragile, fleeting state of balance for our globe,
Allows, wet-nurses a wakefulness,
Within searching souls who question:
Why might, and do, we deserve all this?
Beat all odds, get a cushioned ride?
Others too dense, timid, fearful,
Filled with false pride, or Patricidal hate,
(Perhaps, too P.C. to contemplate
What vast odds appear to indicate).
As Cosmology, Astrophysics, varied
Faiths on converging paths collide.

FATED, SATED, SEPARATED

Nick Kalvin, M.D. ©

A nice pair, I knew, by new, hot love were sated,
Sweaty, spent, ecstatic, each felt lucky, fated,
So much, they Dear-John'd, avoided others,
Told co-workers, fathers, friends and mothers.
Church vows were witnessed, gladly stated.
But, two years later, one mate berated,
"Despite your best touches, I'm no more elated,
Our love's ho-hum, in a downward spin.
Boring, a chore. Nothing like it was in sin."
After the split, found she'd been impregnated.
Judge admonished, "Child-care's mandated,
No matter that once-hot ardor has abated.
You both raise this child right, I do adjure,
Even if costs involved may make you poor!"
This, the Family Court's final paper stated:
Weekly meetings will be strictly regulated;
Kid exchanges throughout each year slated.
In a stiff-lipped fashion, once they began,
Lists, info, son passed between her and the man.
Although re-married, these exes are hooked, related,
Smarter, sadder, by mistake, for life, chained and fated.

ONE SWEET DENTAL ASSISTANT

Nick Kalvin MD ©

A sweet dental assistant named Floss,
Grew an unethical yen for her boss.
Astride his motorized chair,
Scents from her fair, silky hair,
Spurred his drilling with each classy toss.
Beneath his framed, ornate diploma,
They raised a steamy sexual aroma,
Of oozing pheromone sweat
As joined climaxes they'd get.
No doubt, the best oral team in Pomona.
Like an oak keg, with matched, fitted bung,
Measured the same from pubis to tongue.
They clung firmly together,
Tight as braided wet leather,
His feet braced on the lowest chair rung.
Client care went by quickly, because,
By five, she'd sigh, "Oh! Come to me, Ross."
Ending the clinical day,
Launching their nightly sex play.
He paid overtime! What a neat boss!
For years, Floss prayed he'd give her a ring.
That this was not just a sexual thing,
(But Doctor Ross had two wives.
A liar, living three lives,
Used blue pills to avoid faltering).
On a dark, dank day in December,
One which Floss shall always remember.
Her boss seemed very tired,
Mid-stroke, her love expired.
Her clue was his shrinking, deflating member.

When the office goods sale had ended.
Tearful Floss, at last, comprehended,
His used equipment now sold,
That she felt worn out and old,
By two widows, no more befriended.
Gone was the chair which rose and descended,
Where, past sex, they almost transcended.
Now, she had nowhere to go,
But, inside, she'd always know,
She had him last, grandly distended.
To her, that was worth six years expended.

Encouraged by my friend Dr. Boynton, I came to Naples in July 1966, to join 35 bed NCH as the 13th physician and the first eye surgeon in Collier County. The US was still unsettled after the JFK assassination, the Vietnam War, and the JFK legacy Civil Rights Bill. LBJ, confronted by strong Democratic Party opposition, used a unanimous Republican Congressional vote to get full equality for Blacks, especially the South. Like the Civil War, it was Republicans who, once more, freed the Blacks, not the party they so blindly support today.

Dr. Boynton served Collier County School Board in 1967, 68, 69 and 70, the last two years as Chairman. John Murphy was appointed Superintendent. Previously, it was an elected position. The following poem is based on these events and times.

CIVIL RIGHTS IN THE SIXTIES
From LIFE'S NOT FAIR SERIES

Nick Kalvin MD ©

That long ago, Bruce Boynton MD coaxed me to early
Naples, his home town.
Bruce: A scholar, a strong and honest, Christian, most
race-blind man I'd found;
Family Physician; Tither; spent "vacations" doing
charity; kept fees down;
Sang in the church choir; flew Air Patrol for boats in
trouble, at sundown;

Side-line doctor, helped Rotary, Scouts, NCH.
Scolded members of the school board,
Over failure to comply with Civil Rights Acts, which
some locals abhorred.

For years, they'd de-railed action, used politics, covert
coercion and discord.
Many stuck with Old South ways. Sure, this law could
and should be ignored.

Despite Jack Kennedy, and brother, Bob, Civil Rights
had reached a stall,
Until LBJ joined with Republicans to outflank the
Democrat-South cabal.
Angered Dixie die-hards claimed that Kennedy legacy
law was optional.
Enactment shocked separatists. Stirred fear and hate.
Some became irrational.

Bruce's new Board sought Blacks to obey the
measures Congress passed.
Closed all-Black schools, mixing students. For some,
too much, too fast.
Chairman Bruce, his appointed Super, and new Black
official, were all harassed.
Stalked. History reached a turning point and left hard-
shell resistors aghast.

For three men, their wives, came midnight threats.
Sometimes heavy breathing.
One wife, died, a suicide ... upset, afraid of,
depressed by evil unrest seething.
Chairman at times, for order, banged his gavel to
mute rowdy shouts at meeting,
To control those unhinged to see MLK's dream, right
here, right now, bequeathing.

It was sometime later, Bruce called me. "Come to
Outback Acres, if you can,
Need you to evaluate my dear friend, once a
handsome, bright American.
Our first Black Administrator, I recruited for an Acres
school he ran."

On our long drive out, Bruce shared background, and
what happened to this man.

The patient's state was fall-out from storm clouds of
hateful, resentful feeling,
"A Black man in management!" The words set
backwoods, old ways minds to reeling.
There were whispers. Hints of some dark scheme
deniers might be concealing.
(Turned out, perhaps, a midnight ambush, from which
there'd be no appealing).

Bruce thought thugs, tipped to meetings this teacher
would be attending,
On a dark, rural road, blocked his car. What took
place after, past comprehending.
Days later, concerned, a wife phoned Bruce, when
her man's trip became unending.
Bruce back-tracked. Found him at a poor all-Black
clinic. His condition, heart rending.

In his house, this once hale man failed to see light,
even when I'd amplify,
Turn dials, gently, directly, to damaged globes, my
brightest beams apply.
Corneas, milky, hazy, like some I'd seen in training.
Maybe, splashed with lye?
I found low pressures. Diagnosed old, total retinal
detachments of each eye,

I touched scarred skin. Fingered cracked socket rims,
flattened malar eminence,
Suture marks, a boxer's nose. Countless proofs of
impacts and a terrible experience,
He was missing teeth. Sadly, no treatment then (or
now), for his blind dependence.
His battered face, to us, a monument. A living relic of
Old Ways' intransigence.

242

I took his hand. "Sir, it is too late, and injuries too bad,
to get back your eyesight.
But, if your eyes get painful, I'm four blocks north of
Naples only traffic light."
The gentle martyr nodded. Blessed me. Gripped my
hand and held it tight.
Over tea and snacks we sat. We talked. A lot. Bruce
and I got home late that night.

MASSACRE AT HOOP SPUR CHURCH, ARKANSAS 1919

From LIFE'S NOT FAIR SERIES

Nick Kalvin, MD ©

It happened in 1919, in rugged, wooded, rich-soiled eastern
Arkansas.
It was where, along the old Hoop Spur rail line, just north
of Elaine,
Black adult and child farmers in huge fields were all train
riders saw,
In hot sun, bent with burlap sacks, one after another, sweat-
soaked human chain.
The grand Fourteenth Amendment had been passed in
1868,
Signed by both North and South, (called John Bingham's
Bill),
It said that any state in the nation could not discriminate,
Strip people of any color of any rights nor constrict their
free will.

The President, himself, was charged to enforce this new
Bill of Rights.
In cases where states might refuse or fail to make those
laws fit,
Practiced prejudice, the White House resident would make
things right.
So much blood, North and South, spilled in Lincoln's war,
had paid for it.
Two years later, 1870, the Fifteenth Amendment came to
pass.
It granted ballot box access to all voters, regardless of creed
and race.
The Civil Rights Bill of '75 declared, since all men were
one class,

The fact granted free and open access of public places, to any color face.

Eloquent Freedom Fighter, Frederick Douglas, was elated by it all,
Talked of open doors to a color-blind paradise, now availed.
But, the Klan, some poor and wealthy whites, still saw dark Aboriginals.
"Sainted" Woodrow Wilson went off the track, segregated IRS and US Mail.
Harvard's Dean observed, "There's nothing here wrong, for me to call."
While he and Southern Democrats planned to undermine it all,
Colleges published Research "proving" why Blacks were less cerebral,
A view boosted by a new art form, the Minstrel Show Chorale.

In Reconstruction, Blacks were free to go, poor, hungry. Left on their own.
Rented seed, tools, farms. Planted, reaped and sold. Gave thanks and knelt.
Former slave owners turned landlords, amazed to find new expenses low.
Bought Black crops cheap. Then sold high. More profit across the Sun Belt.
Around the world, cloth demand went up. Cotton bale bids to new highs arose!
Black farmers watched it happen. They talked, met three times at Hoop Spur Church,
Formed a new Lodge-Union, voted that a new, co-op cotton price be proposed,
Even, as armed thugs arrived, crept through the Weeping Birch.

The hopeful, peaceful meeting ended in panic. Shots from
countless guns,
Sun-baked Church planks splintered. The few Blacks with
arms did fire back,
Mostly, members, who still could, headed for swamps and
dense woods, on the run.
Next day, an angry Governor Brough ordered his State
Troopers to attack.
Out-manned and out-gunned, Black farmers and kin were
hunted down.
Whole families taken. Shot, beaten, burned, lynched or
jailed over several days.
Brough's machine-gun squads, hoping Lodge leaders
would be found,
Prowled the woods. Found piles of bodies, mass lynching
on forays.

Hundreds died...Some, recently celebrated as World War I
heroes
Had come back home, had just wanted a decent price for
their cotton crop.
For two weeks, air laden with smoke from scattered fires. A
burnt-flesh stench arose
Left behind, in the bullet-riddled, now empty Hoop Spur
Church whistle stop.
Were the new, bold Lodge motto, by-laws, duties,
privileges and member rights,
Little comfort to captured Blacks. Estimated eight hundred,
in jail.
Little Rock now blamed for un-leashed, quick-fingered,
armed state might.
Blacks, their lawyers pleaded for the expected White House
rescue, to no avail.

Seventy-five Lodge members, who survived, were given
prison terms,
Their twelve officers dealt the electric chair, from grim-
faced, all-White juries.

Most charges, however, later, dismissed, as lies and torture
were confirmed,
Proving beyond all doubt, the Federal Investigators' worst-
case worries.
Feds said Black farmers' peacefully founded their Hoop
Spur Lodge-Union,
Its aspirations were never illegal, nor, logically, a single
threat to Whites,
Blacks had merely followed Congress' latest law, and U.S.
Constitution.
Their own state ignored both. Crushed much more than
hard-won, civil rights.

SAN FRANCISCANS WANT SKIN IN THE GAME
(REFERENDUM TO BAN CIRCUMCISION, 2014)

Nick Kalvin, MD ©

Gays there pushed a referendum to ban all circumcisions,
Under age eighteen, even if they're advised by physicians.
Parental choice, to be neutered by one group's proposition,
Fuzzy, Left-Coast Progressive thought trumping wise
clinicians.

Tight or long foreskins often cause weird penile
inflammations,
By yeasts and bacteria feasting on smegma, in such conditions.
A fact long known to old family docs and most pediatricians.
Yet, the movement would ban under-eighteen OR
requisitions,

Despite news that anti-viral benefits come with circumcisions:
Reduced HIV risk, for BOTH sexes, now proven by
statisticians,
Penile and cervical HPV-caused cancer odds, lowered, in
addition.
All of it true, not back-woods, unfounded Conservative
supposition.

For decades, Docs have observed STDs are reduced by
circumcision.
That lucky girls, who, by chance, pick a man with
circumcision
Lower chances of pelvic cancers within one-partner, wedded
coition.
Chaste, honest Nuns spared if they live up to promised
prohibition.

248

Across the globe, Penile cancer is an ugly, even fatal
condition.
Among high-risk takers and those who ignore daily sanitation.
Tomorrow's male babies, who would be denied this minor
operation,
In later life, as in Non-Muslim Asia may face penile
amputation.

At Happy Hour, use the word "foreskin," and you may face
derision,
Unless you're a new Mom, Gay, nurse or practice as a
physician.
Circumcision is a healthy choice. Much more than some
religious tradition.
Proponents of this ban, apparently, have suspended their
cognition.

Why promote this insane, risky, backwards, legal imposition?
Marchers to Protect the Prepuce expose their thinking brains'
inanition.
Soccer Mom and Gays parade to save infant foreskins from
circumcision.
Yet, as to killing unborn siblings, upset if anyone else utters an
objection!

Center for Disease Control is "out," for male infant
circumcisions,
As are leaders in the American Academy of Pediatricians.
What could be the covert motive for this weird and dumb
petition?
Who's offended by the thought of wide-spread prepuce
omissions?
Who yearns for young, intact recruits? Well, I've got my
suspicions.
Folks who prefer and protect down-low, "Foreskin-French"
renditions.

THE BIOLOGIC BLOSSOM FROM DARK DEPTHS
(This image, discovered during a colonoscopy, inspired the poem below.)

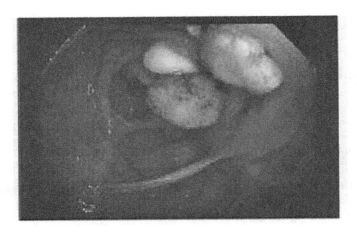

EXPLORING DARK DEPTHS

Nick Kalvin MD ©

I stare at beautiful color photographs
Taken where sunlight's never been
Images remind of some I've seen
On Science Channel and National Geo
Growing about and on the oceans'
Volcanic belching chimney vents
Polypoid, flower-like, multi-lobed
Mine bloom in a concentrating olio
Leaning in a one-way tidal flow
Rife with hydrogen sulfide, other noxious gasses
Limp plant-fibers, grease, rotting remnants
I see three clusters, fringed bivalves half open
One teasingly exposes an ovoid,

Yolk-yellow, pearl-like structure
The trio makes a perfect 4 cm bouquet
Seemingly with a common stem
Amazed to see what can grow, survive
Steeped in borborygmic stinky stew
Someplace below my heart
Who could guess that recent
Dip in routine Hemoglobin
Would result in museum quality
Ascending Colon photographic art
Now, time to find out what we do.

I LOVE MY GENES, ETERNAL MEMORY

Nick Kalvin MD ©

Dear kids, on this birthday, I give thanks for my DNA,
That ingenious protein blend, which got me here today.
Lines of code in woven helix pairs, molded me this way,
An adapting, amino acid mix, traceable to Eve, some say.

So, you see, a long pedigree lives on in all my cells.
This tree branch, as a tiny bud, began with wedding bells,
A cocktail from my Mom's and Dad's genetic wells,
Once the fastest sperm and ripened ovum blended gels.

It's awesome that what-makes-me began long, long ago,
Bits from many, many brave souls, whom I'll never know,
A long line of people, stretching back in history's row,
Their couplings beat unimagined odds, let my future zygote
grow.

Those determined humans who grew up to reproduce,
Despite harsh and scary ages, anthropologists have
deduced,
Fought heat, cold, droughts, disease, fanged creatures on
the loose,
Tamed fire, chipped flint, learned which foods to choose.

The less adept died young. They could not avoid nor rebuff
Early deaths, leaving yours and mine, the clever and the
tough.
To begin primitive clans and all tribes, they were enough.
While scarred elders passed on both learned and biologic
stuff.

Ancient spirit and courage runs through my veins today.

So, family let's toast to my brave kin, who led the early
way.
To those here, progeny to come, my deep respect I convey.
To the vanished of many yesterdays, thank you for great
DNA.

I tell you family, I'm a walking, talking tombstone. Indeed,
A genetic heraldry brandished by every drop I bleed.
So, as towards life's hazards, problems, you all proceed,
Be inspired by, thankful for, our past kindred who did
succeed.

These words are tribute to kinfolk placed in a dark, terrible
pre-history:

Scratching, fighting, hunting, foraging, observing, mating, inventing (flint tools, spears, axes, arrows, fire, pottery, planting grains, uses for fur, cloth and hides). The unsuccessful or conquered: Starved, frozen, eaten, killed by germs, trapped in bogs, killed in combat, some sacrificed prior to reproductive age. We persist, enjoy this gift of life on a wonderful, lonesome, fragile planet, in a vast galaxy. One of billions. We owe existence to tough, courageous, intelligent, wonderful ancestors and their Divine Creator.

Their "genetic memory" is inside us, makes us, drives us. Two thousand years ago, Saints, Disciples, formulated funeral rites, ending with the words, "Grant them Eternal Memory." An amazing, coincidental insight it was, considering Bronze-Copper Age culture of the day. Same words on tombstones of my father, his father, his grandfather, all cantors in the Byzantine Catholic Church, also, unseen, etched in my DNA.

In a sense, we are walking, talking, thinking, biologic tombstones, exploring our own-time world. Each breath, a blessing.

A Thank-You Note
E. J. Noyes

To you, whose hands' life-work has been to carve out evil cancers
from where these find their growing grounds in unsuspecting ears and
necks,
and noses, cheeks and throats;

To you, whose hands gave comfort, trust and hope to hands of those
in need of healing   surgery and strength to carry on;

To you, whose hands were loathe to yield the dear hand of your
much-loved wife to the sterner grip of death;

I wish to say,
I'm deeply touched to have your hand reach out for mine.

March, 2017)

Once Again - But Nicer?
E. J. Noyes

I wish life were nicer.
I wish you'd been nicer;
And I wish I'd been much nicer too - to you.

But now that it's over,
Can we start over,
Just as if you and I have just met?
'Cos for me, there is no one but you.

Perhaps if we try it
Once more, we may like it,
And life may become nicer too.

It should not have been over,
So can we start over?
As if you and I have just met?
'Cos for me, there is no one but you.

(2017)

.

255

About the Author

Elisabeth. J. Noyes

Elisabeth J. Noyes is a writer of poetry and literary criticism, and a Florida Southwestern State College professor of English. Poems of hers have been published in *INPRINT* (a Northshore Community College literary publication), *The Portsmouth Daily Herald* (Portsmouth, NH),and the Southern New Hampshire University *JOURNAL,* since renamed *AMOSKEAG: the Journal of SNHU,* among other publications. Her professional experience includes faculty positions at the college and university level, senior academic administrative positions at Massachusetts and New Hampshire College and University campuses, and senior administrative positions at the Massachusetts and New Hampshire state system boards of public higher education.

Elisabeth Noyes is also recognized for many years of leadership in publicly elected community positions, among which are positions of School Board member (Shirley, MA, eight years), of School Board Chair (three years), and of Town Moderator (Shirley, MA, eighteen years). She has served—and still serves—on various boards of Trustees and boards of Directors of institutions and associations.

A strong believer in life-long learning of experiences of all types, especially those focused on language, literature, art, and education, she holds a M.A. in German Language and Literature from the University of Massachusetts at Amherst; a M.Ed. from Salem State College, Salem, MA; an Ed.D. from Nova Southeastern University, FL.; as well as a M.A. in English from Clark University, Worcester, MA, a degree she earned relatively late, in 2007, and which she values highly.

She is a full-time resident of Marco Island, living happily in the same condominium that she and her husband bought in 1984, and enjoyed for many years as a second home.

FOG HORN

Virginia Colwell Read

Fog horn in the night
Measured call to ships at sea
Through the murk obscuring sight

Fog horn in the night
Breaking through the silent space
To warn of danger in this place

Fog horn in the night
Lonely sentinel in the dark
Guiding ships beyond the mark

Fog horn in the night
Measured call to ships at sea
Assuring safe passage until daylight.

LUNCH IN TOWN

Virginia Colwell Read

We came together

To exchange pleasantries,

To drink and dine with merriment.

We discussed babies, business, and banalities.

The hour was late before we left.

Our hearts were lighter, our burdens less.

The world unchanged.

The Kiss

We walk on a nature trail and smell the loamy soil.
Ferns, green and leafy, are everywhere.

A fallen log is the perfect place to stop and look out over a
lake.
I feel your fingers under my chin; to bring my lips to yours.

You take full advantage as my lips part.
Tenderness envelops me and deepens the kiss.

Your strong hands are on my shoulders.
I look at your burly frame and your handsome face.

Passion overwhelms me.
Your full lips press into mine.

I wonder, am I in love with you?
We stroll, hand in hand.

Your hands are warm and smooth.
We cross a small stream on scattered large stones.

And float back to the car.

By Kristine Taylor
August 7, 2017

Monet's Water Lilies

Kristine Taylor, 2017©

The muted reds, greens, cobalt blues, whites and purples
seem to be floating.
One's eye is drawn to the lily pads.

In another painting, golds, pinks, and greens dance before
your eyes.
A light touch of red flowers sings a solo of dignity.

Yet another shows cobalt blues, yellows, reds and whites.
Black willows weep along the edges.

In the fourth painting, purples, greens and cerulean blues
come alive.
A touch of red stands out on the page.

I Love You, Dad

Kristine Taylor August 7, 2017

You've given me such a high quality of life.
Our outings are so fun.
I enjoy your personality.

Faith draws me in.
Reminds me to pray.
Makes me laugh.

Whether its playing golfing, dining out, or searching for
treasures in thrift stores.
Makes my life enjoyable.
Keeps me on budget.

We go to concerts.
Like Brit Floyd.
Life is good.

Your cooking is always delicious.
Try many new recipes.
I like tasting your different dishes.

So high-tech.
Solve my computer problems.
Help with my projects.
I am grateful.
You are always there for me.

Made in United States
Orlando, FL
13 February 2025

58515404R00154